I0505727

Your Journey   to

REAL   Financial *Freedom*

begins here...

REAL FINANCIAL FREEDOM

by Engr. Myra Almilla

Copyright © 2023
All rights reserved.
ISBN: 9798645163242

Cover Design: Engr. Flora Mae Santos

Published by: Life Coach International Japan

Book Recommendation from Every Nation Pastors and Missionaries

There are many things written about the Christian perspective about money and finance. So, you might think, "Why do we need another such book?" But as I read through my friend Myra's book I was greatly impressed by her style and content. I could feel her passion and empathy to help others. Regular, hard-working, conscientious, and practical people like her and her husband. With great clarity she has been able to show the Bible's principles, practical modern life examples, and very good advice.

Myra and her family have been a part of our church in Yokohama. They live the truths that are presented in this book. I recommend this book for all ages, but especially for the young person just starting out in their career. It will help you make Godly choices that will not only bless you but cause you to be a great blessing to the world around you.

Scott Douma, Senior Pastor
Every Nation Church Yokohama

Reading this book doesn't just make you wise on how to handle your finances but more importantly I admired how it emphasized that your finances should be revolving where finances actually originated, God. I love how it focuses not on the branches but mainly on the roots why we even face financial difficulties at times. I recommend this book not only to those who are clueless on how they should handle their finances; but also, to those who think they already know how to manage them. It's a good way not just to learn new things but also to check your heart and hopefully unlearn wrong mindsets and practices. Consider this book as a blessing because it teaches one not only to be rich but more importantly how to stay intact with your integrity as you become rich.

Dan Encarnacion, Senior Pastor
Every Nation Church Kyrgyzstan

I found it very encouraging and led by God! This book is a great encouragement to me in the area of finances. Myra backs each principle by the Word of God, reminding us of God's heart for us in the area of finances. This book will challenge you and encourage you to take immediate SMART steps to improve your finances. May it be an encouragement to many more!

Yujiro Takagi, Missionary
Every Nation Church Romania

TABLE OF CONTENTS

INTRODUCTION

While writing my book and thinking about its title, I realized that many are already in the business of teaching financial freedom and so I asked myself, what sets it apart from the rest? The heart of this book is not only about financial literacy on its surface. The main goal of writing this book comes from the passion not only to alleviate the readers' economic condition but to elevate their understanding toward the holistic concept of real financial freedom which I believe starts by knowing the true source of everything which is God who is the creator of heavens and the earth. It is followed by knowing the principle of stewardship, establishing the right mindset, breaking bad financial habits, learning how to grow money, and become not only financial literate but prudent in handling finances. Most importantly, knowing the purpose of being financially blessed which is to be a blessing!

I believe that it is God's will for us to be financially free...but what is real financial freedom? This book will allow you to understand real financial freedom and enlighten your heart and mind with the true essence of being blessed and free!

Disclaimer: *Although most of the circumstances in this book were addressed mainly to the financial situation of many Filipino families, the principles presented in this book are biblical; and hence, can be applied by anyone who needs real financial freedom.*

ACKNOWLEDGEMENT

To my Lord and Savior Jesus Christ, the Anchor of my Soul and the Author and Finisher of my faith, I would like to dedicate this book. Apart from you, I am nothing. It's only because of your grace and unwavering, unchanging love that I was able to finish this masterpiece. Thank you for loving me unconditionally.

To my husband and kids who serve as my inspiration, my love, and my pride, may this book continue to remind us that we are indeed blessed because God is with us, and we will continue to love and serve God because He loved us first. Thank you for all the love and support you have given me. I will be forever grateful for your presence in my life.

To our family, friends, loved ones, and mentors, whom God used to shape and mold me to be the person that I am now, thank you very much. You will always be treasured and loved. I am blessed because you came into my life.

To you who are now holding this book, thank you for giving your precious time to read it. It's my prayer that none of those times will be wasted; instead, they will be multiplied and produce good fruits in your life. It is my pleasure to be part of your journey.

ABOUT THE
Author
AND HER HEART

Hi! I'm Myra and I'm from the Philippines.

I finished my Bachelor's degree in Civil Engineering from Mapua Institute of Technology and graduated as Cum Laude. Meanwhile, I received my Master's degree in Business Administration from Globis University in Tokyo, Japan and was among the top-performing graduates in my class.

I have significant years of experience in the corporate world and worked for well-known Japanese Companies like Japan Gas Corporation (JGC) and Chiyoda Corporation whose main expertise lies in the construction of oil and gas facilities which are responsible for producing the world's fuel and other energy resources. My exposure to the corporate world has honed me to be the responsible, excellent, and service – oriented person that I am right now. Through time, I was able to learn the proper way of handling financial blessings from our Lord. And since I was not born from a rich family, I seek His wisdom in the area of finance; and God is faithful, when He said He gives wisdom to those who ask Him. God has shaped my heart into the understanding of what Real Financial Freedom is all about. That it's not the abundance of money, but the pursuit of His kingdom and His righteousness in the field of finance.

I am aware of the Philippines' economic condition and I myself have seen and tasted poverty and its sting. I know how it is to live from one place to another and ask one relative after the other to seek for shelter. I know all the struggles a commuter faces each day just to get home using public transportations and I know how it is to choose between traversing the precarious highway or take the unlighted overpass during the night because those were the only options I have. Oh yes! Looking back... it was hard; but amid all those challenging situations, I knew I had a choice and I learned how to soar.

I am now living with my family in Japan and we are doing well. We have been blessed and continue to be a blessing to others as well. All these things became possible because of our faithful God; nothing more, and nothing less.

The path I walked on may not be as straight as I would have planned it, but God in His abundant grace showed me mercy and lighted my once dark road and led me as to where I am right now.

I have read several books on finance that are really good and seem very effective because the author himself is a picture that depicts riches and abundance; and to most, this is financial freedom. However, I knew in my heart that if we really want to pull our lives together and experience real financial freedom, we should seek first the One who is the owner of everything. We must acknowledge His authority over our wealth and recognize that we are nothing but stewards of his abundant grace. My desire is that you will be able to discern from God his good, pleasing, and perfect will. I believe that if we seek him with all our heart, mind, and soul, he will add unto us everything, and that includes our financial well-being!

May this book richly bless you in every way!

FOREWORD

Let me give you some advice as you read this book.

1. *I AM NOT PERFECT*

I am not perfect and still a work in progress in the area of finance. I am also in the continuous process of cultivating myself with other resources to enhance my understanding and skills on this matter. Nonetheless, I am thankful to be used by God and share with you some of the lessons I have learned through time. I am hoping that upon reading this book, your eyes will be opened, and you will continue to develop a habit of educating yourself to improve your financial well-being.

2. *THIS BOOK IS NOT THE ANSWER TO ALL YOUR FINANCIAL PROBLEMS*

I am hoping that this book will strengthen you and your faith that there is an option and a way out of financial chaos. Reading this book does not mean an end mean to resolve your current situation. You must realize that an action must be taken and there is a decision to be made and a commitment to set that you will get out of your financial mess and will have to plan how to make it in order. In other words, the way to real financial freedom is a process and you will need to exert some effort from your side.

3. MONEY IS NOT EVERYTHING AND EVERYONE HAS A DIFFERENT CALLING

I strongly hope that your number one goal for reading this book is not how to make more money and live life to the fullest. I wrote this book to emphasize the love of God for you even in the area of finance. That real financial freedom is having peace and joy with what God has blessed you with and living as a good steward of God's entrusted resources by putting it in order and growing it so you can be a channel of God's grace. I desire that after reading this book you will no longer compare your economic status with other people. That you will have the confidence that God is doing something in your behalf, He wants to bless you, and He has a unique calling for you.

Experiencing real financial freedom is not dependent on how much money you're earning and it's never about your starting position in life or society. It's mostly a combination of knowledge, wisdom, and understanding of how well you can manage the resources that are being entrusted to you. Yes, you got it right – entrusted resources! Because everything that we have all comes from One Source – the Creator of Heaven and Earth!

We need to understand that we are only Stewards of His great mercy and grace – and that includes our finances!

Let us then go through this book by this principle, "our God loves us so much and He wants to bless us abundantly more than we can ever think or imagine"; however, this is a matter of the heart. And when it comes to the matter of the heart, there should always be a change of mindset.

Do not conform to the pattern of this world, but be transformed by the renewing of your mind. Then you will be able to test and approve what God's will is—his good, pleasing, and perfect will.
(Romans 12:2 – NIV)

We must be willing to have our eyes fixed on what really matters and be willing to change our habits in ways that pleases God and align our will with His. This is the start of every new great thing. It is only when we seek the Blesser and the purposes of God that real blessings overflow in our lives.

But seek first his kingdom and his righteousness, and all these things will be given to you as well. (Matthew 6:33 – NIV)

Let me encourage you to start putting your finances in order by establishing your faith that God has already provided everything that you need for you to live your destiny! May this book allow God to move in your life in ways you have never experienced before, and may you have a time of refreshing as you make your steps toward Real Financial Freedom!

Chapter 1

WHAT IS REAL FREEDOM?

So if the Son sets you free, you are truly free.
(John 8:36 – NLT)

So how can you say that someone is free? Are the rich free? Or should someone say, "When I get rich, then I will be free". Definitely no! There are a lot of rich people who are not free, unhappy and in bondage. If they do, there should never be a newspaper column dedicated to the rich and famous who committed suicide due to depression. Who then are free? Real and perfect freedom comes from the One who sets us free – and that is Jesus, the Son of God. Freedom does not mean we can always do anything we want when we want it. Genuine Freedom is when we can boldly say NO to the stuff that are non-beneficial to us. When we no longer struggle in doing the things that will only do us harm rather than good and hurt us, our loved ones, and our Creator. God has great and wonderful plans for us. Poverty is not from God. It is a bondage and a cycle that will never end – all because of sin. It is also a result of our poor choices in life!

There will always be poor people in the land
(Deuteronomy 15:11 – NIV)

Nonetheless, God is our redeemer. We may have chosen otherwise; however, God is not troubled. He will never stammer because of our imprudent judgments. He knows exactly what to do even if we messed up.

I am not saying that if you surrender to God now and accept Jesus in your life, you will be free from all your debts and live a great life. A life of surrender means giving God the opportunity to intervene in your affairs; and for all we know, once God intervene, we can expect better results.

Real financial freedom, hence, is not only having the abundance of money; it is however, a life that is no longer struggling with money or regularly hardly making both ends meet and being able to sleep peacefully each night because you know that tomorrow is taken care of. It's a lifestyle, so to speak. A way of life where savings, investments, and passive income is no longer a dream but a reality because you know exactly what stewardship is all about. Above all, it is a life that is full of purpose because you know that at the end of the day, you are God's workmanship that was created for His every good deed where you will always choose to make a difference in somebody else's life and serve as a channel of blessing in every occasion so that all your good works may result in thanksgiving to God.

POVERTY IN THE PHILIPPINES

Blessed is the nation whose God is the LORD,
the people he chose for his inheritance.
(Psalm 33:12 – NIV)

Philippines, as we claimed it as the most prominent Christian Nation in Asia in its essence is a blessed Nation indeed; however, it cannot be concealed that it also perfectly depicts the picture of poverty. From the National government down to its governing provinces and cities, we can see the devastating condition of poor Filipinos. Meanwhile, just upon the takeover of every Administration, the GDP (Gross Domestic Product) was claimed to reach increase which hovered against the reign of previous administrations; furthermore, in some publications concerning economic growth, Philippines was considered as the Rising Tiger of Asia in the international community.

On the contrary, the average Juan Dela Cruz remains unconvinced of the economic growth that was being presented through the Stocks tickler and other indicators. All he knows is that there are sweltering stomachs among his children and that even a descent shelter is beyond his reach. "Good Education and Healthcare Facilities are for the rich", he says. Every media survey says that according to an average Filipino, he has never felt the change and poverty is still before his very face. As of this writing and according to the government's recent data, about a quarter of the population lived below the National poverty line. Unfortunately, a huge percentage of marriages failed because of financial reasons; on top of that, there are Filipinos who have not attained their financial independence upon reaching their retirement and hence, most of them depend on their children for support during their old age. Furthermore, there are senior citizens who failed to save enough money and find themselves needing to work beyond the superannuation age for food and maintenance medicine. On the other hand, there are also married couples who opted to stay with their parents because they have not prepared for their life as a couple by which several conflicts arise among in-laws. Why is it that a Nation who claims to be having Jesus as Lord is now suffering from this shattering reality? Why is it that until now, some Filipinos are still within or below the poverty line?

This is what the LORD of Heaven's Armies says: Look at what's happening to you! You have planted much but harvest little. You eat but are not satisfied.

You drink but are still thirsty. You put on clothes but cannot keep warm. Your wages disappear as though you were putting them in pockets filled with holes!
(Haggai 1:5-7 – NLT)

God is in control of everything. He can command blessings and curses in our lives and over a nation. And because the people of Israel, even if they were a chosen nation did not consider putting God on top of their priorities during that time, they were cursed. In view thereof, our priorities should be set and realigned with the TRUTH which is the unchanging and infallible Word of God.

As contrary to what the world teaches about wealth, let us see how the Word of God elucidates the proper perspective that we should be applying to our own finances.

Worldly *vs.*

Godly Thinking on Finances

The Reality is...

Money is the root of all evil, so it is better to stay poor because having a lot of money is a sin.

The Truth is...

**For the love of money is the root of all kinds of evil.
(1Tim 6:10 – NLT)**

It is not money which is the root of all evil; rather, it is the love of money, which means, loving something will compel you to do everything in your ability to preserve it. This includes going against the will of God.

The Reality is...

Giving means losing on my part.

The Truth is...

**It is more blessed to give than to receive.
(Acts20:35 – NLT)**

Give and it will be given to you. A good measure, pressed down, shaken together and running over, will be poured into your lap. For with the measure you use, it will be measured to you. (Luke 6:38 – NIV)

One person gives freely, yet gains even more; another withholds unduly, but comes to poverty.
(Proverbs 11:24 – NIV)

Giving would never strip us of anything except our greed and pride. This only means that we are essentially sowing something which we will eventually reap in time. A farmer knows this very well.

<u>The Reality is...</u>

Tithing and giving love gifts only show a picture of innocence among church members and connivance among the Church Leaders to serve their own financial growth.

<u>The Truth is...</u>

Bring the whole tithe into the storehouse, that there may be food in my house. Test me in this," says the LORD Almighty, "and see if I will not throw open the floodgates of heaven and pour out so much blessing that there will not be room enough to store it.
(Malachi 3:10 – NIV)

Tithing is in fact an act of worship before God. Knowing that He owns everything, it is technically more proper to say that tithing is not giving to God but GIVING BACK TO GOD. We do not give back with blindfolds in our eyes and we do not bring the tithes into the storehouse to serve our leaders, but because we love God, we have experienced transformation in our lives, and we strongly believe in the faithfulness of His promises.

Each of you should give what you have decided in your heart to give, not reluctantly or under compulsion, for God loves a cheerful giver. (2Corinthians 9:7 – NLT)

It does not mean that God loves only those who can give; remember that our actions can never shift the nature of God. This only means that God delights in our giving. God will never compel us to give something that will not benefit us. It has always been His will to bless us and increase us in every aspect of our lives – and this includes our finances.

The Reality is...

It is ok to be in debt... like most people in the world.

The Truth is...

For even the Son of Man did not come to be served, but to serve, and to give his life as a ransom for many. (Mark 10:45 – NIV)

Jesus, in His human form paid the biggest debt humanity has ever had by dying on the cross. How could this ever mean that God would want you to live your life with so many liabilities? God wants you to be debt free!

The Reality is...

It is just fine to find luck in the lottery or casino; who knows, I might win the jackpot and go big time!

The Truth is...

Dishonest money dwindles away, but whoever gathers money little by little makes it grow. (Proverbs 13:11 – NIV)

All hard work brings a profit, but mere talk leads only to poverty. (Proverbs 14:23 – NIV)

As practical as it seems, owning something which you did not work for will only put you in a precarious situation, leaving you confused and wondering how to manage the resources which you never had before or which you were uneducated to handle. It is better to go through the process of building wealth slowly but surely. Doing hard work in building wealth and continuously educating yourself on proper financial management will help you to live the best life God has intended for you.

The Reality is...

I have the right to do whatever I want with my wealth because I was the one who worked hard for it.

The Truth is...

The earth is the LORD's, and everything in it, the world, and all who live in it. (Psalm24:1 – NIV)

But remember the LORD your God, for it is he who gives you the ability to produce wealth... (Deuteronomy 8:18 - NIV)

The truth is, we were all born with nothing! When we land on earth, all we have is the breath that God has given us.

Every ability that enables us to produce wealth is the Lord's; hence, it is only appropriate for us to acknowledge that everything belongs to Him. We should honor Him by doing what He wants us to do with the wealth that He has entrusted to us.

The Reality is...

Remaining poor while serving God is a sign of meekness and humility.

The Truth is...

You shall not muzzle an ox while it treads out the grain," and, "The laborer is worthy of his wages." (1 Timothy 5:18 – NKJV)

Moreover, when God gives someone wealth and possessions, and the ability to enjoy them, to accept their lot and be happy in their toil—this is a gift of God. (Ecclesiastes 5:19 – NIV) "

The Word clearly tells us that it is not God's will to put a muzzle in his servant's mouth. Instead, He wants us to be prosperous as we serve Him. He rejoices with us as we enjoy His blessings while we worship Him through our service.

The list may go on and on and on.... The bible has so much to say about our finances and the way we should handle them. God is so much concern about your well-being and He knows the answer to every question you have in mind concerning the management of your earthly resources. All you need to do is believe that He wants to bless you exceedingly and abundantly more than you can ever think or imagine!

Keep this Book of the Law always on your lips; meditate on it day and night, so that you may be careful to do everything written in it. Then you will be prosperous and successful. (Joshua 1:8 - NIV)

The choice is yours and the question is – are you willing to accept His guidance for your success?

GENERATIONAL CURSES

It may be clear and obvious for a nation to be in an impoverished condition; however, this is only one of the many factors that affect one's personal economic condition. Have you ever heard of generational curses? The bible speaks clearly that as blessings can be passed down from generation to generation, and so are curses.

Your basket and your kneading trough will be cursed.18 The fruit of your womb will be cursed, and the crops of your land, and the calves of your herds and the lambs of your flocks.38 You will sow much seed in the field but you will harvest little, because locusts will devour it. 39 You will plant vineyards and cultivate them but you will not drink the wine or gather the grapes, because worms will eat them. 40 You will have olive trees throughout your country but you will not use the oil, because the olives will drop off. 41 You will have sons and daughters but you will not keep them, because they will go into captivity. 42 Swarms of locusts will take over all your trees and the crops of your land.
(Deuteronomy 28:17~18, 38~42 – NIV)

You must identify whether poverty is in your bloodline. Like any disease which can be transmitted through offspring and recognized by science as hereditary, poverty can also be inherited. Growing up, you probably wonder why you often struggle financially and why you were in constant poverty. You have seen it first in your parents; then, your siblings. You were taught that finishing a degree in college will give you a better life; and here you are, working so hard and sweating it all, but still, trying to make both ends meet on a regular basis. There are times when you will experience abundance; but in just a snap of a finger, at a wink of an eye, somebody will get sick, and all that you have suddenly...is gone. It may not be sickness; but for one reason or another, all life's circumstances often look unfavorable on your side and you seem to put your money in a torn basket that never fills up no matter how hard and desperate you try. If you are that person, seeing poverty passed down from one generation to another, there is no doubt that poverty runs in your blood. Today, you must decide to choose freedom and breakthrough is the only option you have. The thing is, you are not the answer; Jesus is! Remember that poverty, a generational curse runs in your blood; and if only you were born in a different family with a different bloodline, it would be different. If only it's possible... The good news is… it is!

You should not be surprised at my saying,
'You must be born again. (John 3:7 – NIV)

See what great love the Father has lavished on us,
that we should be called children of God!
(1John 3:1 – NIV)

And yes, that is who we are – "Children of God",
the moment we put our faith in Jesus! You can have a
different bloodline. A bloodline that is free from the curse
of poverty! The blood of Jesus that was shed on the cross
paid for everything!

When he had received the drink, Jesus said, "It is
finished." With that, he bowed his head and
gave up his spirit. (John 19:30 – NIV)

It is finished and it was paid in full! Your job is to
accept that breakthrough through the finished work of
Jesus Christ on the cross. You can do it by confessing
your faith before God, asking for forgiveness from all your
sins and the sins of your family, and receive the
forgiveness and cleansing of our Lord. Accept Him as
your Lord and Savior. Decide from now on that He will be
in charge of your life; and that includes your finances.
Generational curses are something that can only be cut off
through Jesus Christ and you must decide now.

GETTING OUT OF POVERTY AND LIVING GOD'S DESTINY

Poverty must have been such a universal word which is most visible in all parts of the globe. Everyone is aware of poverty. Even the richest countries in the world are no excuse for this phenomenon.

There will always be poor people in the land...
(Deuteronomy 15:11 – NIV)

And though, the term poverty does not only denote the state of being poor or the lack of money, this is the most evident of all; hence, let us focus on this note. Because we are living in a fallen world, poverty will always be visible everywhere; however, the good news is – Jesus already paid the price for our freedom!

For you know the grace of our Lord Jesus Christ, that
though he was rich, yet for your sake he became poor,
so that you through his poverty might become rich.
(2 Corinthians 8:9 – NIV)

In other words, He nailed it all! And He sealed it with His own blood! Why do I have to reiterate this? Because it is only through the change of mindset that we can truly experience the good things that God has stored for us. Yes, before we can fully enjoy the benefits of all that God has planned for us, we must be convinced that it is only through Him that we can attain real financial freedom and live not only a successful life but also a significant and satisfied one!

For I know the plans I have for you," declares the LORD, "plans to prosper you and not to harm you, plans to give you hope and a future. (Jeremiah 29:11 – NIV)

We must realize that God has a plan... a great plan for us to prosper and experience a wonderful future. Wow! Isn't that so compelling? And yes, when you know that God loves you so much and He has a perfect plan for you, then you can just face anything. And with a cheerful heart, even if it seems a little bit dark, you know that at the end of it is a lighted path that opens to all the possibilities of blessings and favor and grace!

Let us therefore primarily receive from the Lord – the creator of every good and perfect gift!

Prayer: Father God, thank you for your son, Jesus Christ who gave himself as a ransom for my salvation and whom you have sent on the cross to die on my behalf. I ask that you cleanse my heart and forgive me from all my sins.

Today, I receive Jesus Christ in my heart as my Lord and my Savior. From now on, please take charge of my life and my finances. In Jesus Name, Amen.

Congratulations for taking the first step in fixing your finances! I am not saying that everything will be easy from here; but I'm sure, it will be a lot lighter because now, you have God with you in carrying your burdens.

Come to me, all you who are weary and burdened and I will give you rest.
(Matthew 11:28 – NIV)

Chapter 2

THE ROAD TO REAL FINANCIAL FREEDOM

*There is a way that appears to be right
but in the end it leads to death. (Prov14:12 – NIV)*

*But small is the gate and narrow the road that
leads to life, and only a few find it. (Mat7:14 – NIV)*

The road to real financial freedom is narrow and only a few chose this road; however, it leads to life. And a life yielded to God always produces good fruits. In the same way, a financial report surrendered to God will always yield a positive result. The road to real financial freedom is not a quick scheme easy to get rich formula. It is a process which may be extremely difficult and sharply discomforting particularly to someone who will be hearing it for the first time. Nonetheless, take heart, because a tree to fully grow must undergo pruning from time to time; so, kindly consider some pruning process while reading this book.

While writing this book, there were times when I wanted to quit because I felt like I was just wasting my time, and who needs another book on finance anyway? However, after hearing from some of the closest persons to my heart like colleagues and friends, especially the young professionals and OFWs (Overseas Filipino Workers) who are struggling with their finances, I was moved with compassion, and I realized that there was a sense in pursuing this book. While hearing their stories, I perceive that a continuous battle is unfolding, and the outcry for freedom is crucial. When asked why there is a struggle, the answer is simple: they don't know what to do or how to do it appropriately.

Sometimes people even say that the matter of money is taboo, something we should never talk about. Meanwhile, the Bible has several verses written on finance, which serve as proof that these issues are important to God and our attitudes toward them reflect who we truly are and what we truly believe.

This book is a doorway showing you that options are available for improvements and that financial order is possible. We may have been raised differently; but all you need is an open mind and a teachable heart if you really want to succeed in this area. It does not matter how much money you have in your pocket right now. What matters is how much you are willing to pay the costs of getting your finances on track.

RENEWING OF MINDS

I was born in a modest family. It is a family that strongly believes in the power of education. Of getting a college diploma and landing in a good company. I was never trained to have the mindset of an entrepreneur. I was never educated to put my passion into something that can create business and employment for those who cannot create opportunities for themselves. I was never trained to be a millionaire! A totally different program was inputted in my mind as I was growing up. I cannot blame my parents. They are not aware, and they were also raised that way. Nevertheless, thanks be to God! When I came to know the Lord Jesus, I was reprogrammed. My brain was set to a new mode of thinking. I realized that our God is not poor! Our God is rich! Yes, He is rich not only in mercy and grace but in every way and in every area that we can think of! My mind was set to a new level of thinking. I was once living in mediocrity and wrong notion and limitations. God is an unlimited God and He is the source of everything! I began to shift my mind from the thinking of the poor to the thinking of the rich! I started to believe that there is a bright future waiting for me because that's what the Word of God says.

For I know the plans I have for you," declares the LORD,
"plans to prosper you and not to harm you, plans to give
you hope and a future. (Jeremiah 29:11 – NIV)

Sad to say, there are some mentalities that limit our capacity to succeed and prevent financial blessings to flourish which needs reprogramming, a total mind shifting, and upgrading.

THE POOR MENTALITY

1. We Were Born Poor

Yes, this is true; but it doesn't have to be true all the time. You may have been born that way but there are always opportunities and options available for you not to stay in that status quo. God is always opening new doors of opportunities for us to prosper and live a better life. God is always writing a new story in our lives. A new chapter that will bring glory to Him! He may shut one door but for sure He is opening another because our God is a God of progress. What He did for you ten years ago is not as good as what He is doing in the present or about to do in the future.

There is always something greater and brighter and fresher; and that is what I like most about God! He always brings us to a new height of expectations.

He makes my feet like the feet of a deer;
he causes me to stand on the heights.
(Psalm 18:33 – NIV)

When God told us to go to Japan, it was a tough choice because we must leave everything behind. We thought that we already have all that we wanted in the Philippines; our spiritual family, a high paying and satisfying job, loyal friends, and most importantly, our family. But God, in his infinite knowledge and wisdom showed us when we obeyed Him that there are a lot more to see – a lot better than what my husband and I have planned for!

We don't have to live in complacency. Our "This is enough attitude" should be replaced by "What Lord attitude". "Lord what do you want me to accomplish?" We should always be opportunity – seeking people. Those who are always seeking for opportunities to please God and bring Him glory. And being in the state of "we were born poor" mindset is definitely not from Him.

2. Money does not Grow on Trees

Are you familiar with this - *mahirap kumita ng pera, dugo't pawis ang kapalit* (Money is hard to earn; it costs us blood and sweat)!? I heard that several times! I even often heard this one – *hay naku, wala akong kapera pera* (sigh, I have nothing left; not even a penny!) I'm not so sure why it is so easy to declare curses rather than blessings or complains instead of faith? Don't you know that life and death is in the power of tongue?

**Death and life are in the power of the tongue,
And those who love it will eat its fruit.
(Proverbs 18:21 – NKJV)**

Oftentimes, many are unaware of the implications of their declarations especially when their children are the ones who are listening. Afterwards, they wonder why their descendants never seem to alleviate from poverty and never came to a conclusion that it was the result of the program they inputted in their children's mind - that money is hard to earn! So, if you want to change this mindset and never let it sink on the next generation, learn to declare God's blessings instead of curses! Yes, I agree that hard work is required for us to acquire our goals in life but we should never neglect the power that is associated with our confessions. You should motivate *your children by saying, "it's never impossible for you to be successful!" "God has great and wonderful plans for you!" "You will go to greater heights!" "You can soar above all circumstances and blessings will overtake you because our God is alive and He lives forevermore!" Aren't those sound a lot better, right?*

3. Being Rich is a Shame; it's too Ambitious

We Filipinos were trained not to boast. In our language we will say, "wag magbuhat ng sariling bangko" (never lift your own seat) otherwise people might say that we are conceited. And even if it's true, we were just so afraid to receive compliments. Instead of saying "thank you", we often choose to degrade ourselves by saying meek words. For example, a friend would say, "nice shirt", we would say, "this is cheap." Do you see what I mean? Honest compliments need honest responses as well. Why is it so hard to see that there's nothing wrong with accepting praises? You see, this spectacle has a high impact also on our financial well-being. If you are afraid to accept good compliments, how can you accept good things from the Lord as well? "Nakakahiyang maging mayaman" (it's a shame to be rich). We are so afraid to tell other people or even our loved ones about our dreams because we wanted to avoid critical judgements.

41

Furthermore, we fear that we might not get what we dreamed of and they will just laugh at us and leave us embarrassed. Let me tell you, don't be afraid! Dream big dreams! Declare your lot and be a visionary! Don't be afraid of what others have to say. Confess your dreams and believe that nothing is impossible with God! I assure you; dreams do come true! And God has placed a desire in your heart that is so unique that only you can accomplish. Start by delighting yourself in the Lord.

Take delight in the LORD, and he will
give you the desires of your heart.
(Psalm 37:4 – NIV)

It doesn't mean that God will give you everything you want. This means that when you delight in Him, He will supply the desires of your heart. That is, God's desire will be your desire; and for sure, it is the most wonderful because He is God and He knows what's best for you!

4. Success is Not for Me; Others, but Not for Me

Why not? Because it's not in your blood line? Or because you only graduated from high school and never had the chance to go to college? Or maybe because you have never seen anyone in the family who succeeded?

Whatever your excuses are, I assure you that success is for everyone! It's just a matter of asking why and how. Why? It's because God created a conqueror not a loser.

No, in all these things we are more than conquerors through him who loved us.
(Romans 8:37 – NIV)

You were born to be victorious! I have heard, seen, and read so much about self-made millionaires and what makes the difference? They are just mere human beings like us who happen to have the same 24 hours every single day. You want to know the main difference? It's their mindset! The only difference between successful and unsuccessful people is their mindset. A Different mindset leads to a different action which gives a different result. And here is the good news: successful people leave footprints as they walk. This gives us hope that if we can trace the path they have taken, the possibilities become imaginable! Yes, if we can adopt their way of thinking and apply it to our own lives, there is a strong likelihood that we can attain the same level of success they have experienced.

5. It's More Blessed to Receive than Give

Do you know that there's a culture in Japan of give and take? Once somebody gave you a gift, it's polite to give them back something in return. That I think, is a gesture of appreciation, gratitude, and respect. On the other hand, let's say you know a friend who happens to have a restaurant. Instead of thinking of eating there and promoting her restaurant so you can bless her, what you will do is ask her to give you a free dinner. Or say, you know a makeup artist; and instead of getting her service to your wedding so you can bless her, what you will do is ask her if she can make your wedding makeup for free. How many of us can relate? The Word of God is clear...

...it is more blessed to give than to receive.
(Acts 20:35 – NIV)

Again, financial freedom is a matter of the heart. You can always choose to take advantage of other people including your friends and loved ones or trust God to do His will even if it's in contrary to what the world teaches. The choice is yours and I hope that you choose wisely.

6. *One day Millionaire - YOLO (You Only Live Once)*

We are living in Japan and some local channels feature interesting topics about other countries like USA, Europe and occasionally, Philippines. One time, they featured about how different countries treat their money from a salary man's perspective. Salary man in Japan is defined as someone who depends on employment for income. A family of 4 was once featured. And this is what happened. After getting their salary, the family went shopping, bought some nice clothes and toys for the kids and ate in a fancy restaurant until they almost run out of cash. All happened in one day! After that, the show went on by moving to their dwelling place the other day. Meals were served and guess what? They're eating instant noodles this time! Of course, the Japanese hosts were extremely surprised. One commentator said, "In Japan, the mentality is not to use up everything, because we think of the future and the future is uncertain."

We should learn how to look beyond now and see the future; and this poor mentality, thinking that showoffs can make us look rich must be eradicated from our system.

My heart goes out for a lot of OFWs who devoted several years of hard work before going back to the country and then in one day live like real millionaires, spend a lot in giving unlimited drinks, merry making and partying, and then go back to working overseas emptyhanded...

No one can boast about tomorrow and we must learn to live like ants.

Ants are creatures of little strength, yet they store up their food in the summer. (Proverbs 30:25 – NIV)

On the other hand, you can shift those poor mindsets and choose to be blessed. Notice that I used the word blessed rather than rich. This is because I want us to focus on the goodness and mercy of our God rather than our own way of thinking. There are perhaps a lot of rich people but not all of them consider themselves blessed. You may have heard of billionaires who have taken their own lives because of depression, loneliness, or hopelessness; and that is because, acquiring wealth without acknowledging the Source is futile and restless.

4 Do not wear yourself out to get rich; do not trust your own cleverness. 5 Cast but a glance at riches, and they are gone, for they will surely sprout wings and fly off to the sky like an eagle. (Proverbs 23:4-5 – NIV)

Hence, let us focus on having a blessed mentality. The mentality that says, whatever my situation is, I know *that God is doing something behind the curtains, and He will make all things beautiful in His time and that all things work together for good to those who love God and are called according to his purpose.*

THE BLESSED MENTALITY

1. Dreams do Come True

Have you ever dreamed? I did; and I would say, most of them already came true! The first key to having a blessed mentality is to start believing! Begin by cutting off all the lies of defeat that were placed in your mind while growing up; like, "you are born for nothing" or "you will never end up to anything." Put it on the cross of Jesus and start declaring the truth in your life. Speak blessings in your life and believe them! Faith is more than just positive thinking. It is being certain! It's being sure of the things unseen and confident of the things we hoped for.

Start praying for a godly vision and make a vision board of your own and set your goals.

**Where there is no revelation, the people cast off restraint; But happy is he who keeps the law.
(Proverbs 29:18 – NKJV)**

It will be so much easier to see where you are going if you have a concrete visualization of what you want to achieve in life. Never include something on your vision board that is easily attainable. Instead, choose something that will challenge both your abilities and your faith. Otherwise, you will not rely on God. Place it in an area where you will be able to see it as often as you want. Visualize it even more in your mind until all your senses agree with you and cause you to move closer in achieving them.

2. Everyone is Unique and Gifted

Do you know that you have what it takes? That God has deposited an enormous amount of uniqueness and gifting that you can use to live a blessed life and serve as a channel of blessing for other people? Of course, you have them! Believe it! God has blessed you with all the talents and abilities you need to excel in life! If you were programmed differently while growing up, this is the time to shift those wrong thinking into right thinking with God. Believe that there are certain tasks that only you can do and do it so uniquely which can bring so much difference in you and in the life of those that surround you. You are intended to be a channel of blessing. There's no one that has it all! You can always offer something different and useful to other people and you can use them to achieve your goals in life.

3. You Have a Choice and You can Choose to do What You Really Love

Have you ever heard this, "Do what you love so you never have to work for the rest of your life"? I believe that if you are passionate about something that you do, you will produce more fruits. If you are merely waking up each day and continuously dragging yourself out of bed in order to go to your eight-hour regular job just to get by, Oh men! You're wasting your time and your company's resources! If this is you, then the probability is, you're not on the right place at the right time; and if it's true, then, you're not using your gifts and talents at its highest potential. Why don't you look for something that you really love to do? Remember those younger days when all you do is laugh and play. What makes you extravagantly happy? What makes you so enthusiastic that made you late for lunch every time your mother looks for you? Yes, those younger days can help you think of what you really love to do and you can turn that passion into income! Be creative. Educate yourself and think of ways on how you can start your own business. You'll be surprised at how high you can reach. Remember that you have a choice and you can choose to do what you really love to do!

4. Discipline is Powerful

Why is there such a term as 1ˢᵗ world and 3rd world country? I'm not sure until I went to Japan! My first overseas assignment as a Civil Engineer was in the land of the rising sun and even at a first glance, I have seen the difference. Life in Japan is nothing, but all based on a very systematic way. People on escalators and walkalators never have to be told to stay on the left side to give way to other individuals who are walking on a faster phase. No one needs to be reminded to wait until all the passengers in one station alighted before they enter the train. Even the kids on the playground were trained to fall in line and wait for their turn when using the slide or swing or other public facilities. And why is this so? Because that's part of their system - discipline is part of their everyday life! In order to be rich or successful, discipline must be part of the system. Discipline means doing what needs to be done even if it seems unlikely or out of one's comfort zone. Discipline could mean not eating at your favorite restaurant as it would cost you more than your budget and will sidetrack you from your goals. It may also mean not talking to your favorite chat mate in the office for it may incur loss in your productivity and miss your chance of promotion. Or, it can probably mean missing your favorite TV show and choosing to show up in a seminar that would enhance your potential as a businessperson. Discipline may cause us discomfort but gives us tremendous results. It's a trait that should be developed, and once developed, it should be harnessed so it can become a habit; and when it becomes a habit, it will be part of our behavior. And just like the 1st world country I mentioned before, it's part of their system; it produces great and powerful impacts not only to their country, but also to the rest of the world.

5. Successful People are People of more Service

Newton's third law of motion states that for every action (force) in nature there is an equal and opposite reaction. In other words, if object A exerts a force on object B, object B will also exert an equal force on object A. A simpler principle was written,

Give and it will be given to you. A good measure, pressed down, shaken together and running over, will be poured into your lap. For with the measure you use, it will be measured to you. (Luke 6:38 – NIV)

I worked in the corporate world for almost two decades and I have seen the dynamics of several employees toward money and work. Most employees' reason for resignation and tenure is money. Often, their success is equated to the amount of money they generate and most of the time these individuals are those that never find satisfaction in what they do. It's simply because money is their top priority and not their service. If you want increase in whatever area of your life, you must put value in what you do and remember that money is only a byproduct of the value that you provide. Most self-made millionaires make it a priority to ensure the quality of their products and services; thus, producing long-term satisfactory results, business retention, and sustainability. If you want to think like the rich people, you must learn to think of how you can make the world a better place. Most of the strongest businesses in the world started by simply identifying a problem and offering a solution. In a micro perspective, working as an employee would mean producing outputs with the highest quality and sometimes even beyond what is expected. Be of more service; that is, working more than you are being paid for until you can be paid more than what you work for!

GOOD STEWARDSHIP

The only person who was, who is, and who will ever be responsible for your financial growth is no other than you! Whether you will be successful or not is up to you for God has already equipped you with all that you need to succeed in life.

Praise be to the God and Father of our Lord Jesus Christ, who has blessed us in the heavenly realms with every spiritual blessing in Christ. (Ephesians 1:3 – NIV)

What we must understand is that our limited thinking limits us to limited resources: however, **WITH GOD ALL THINGS ARE POSSIBLE!** *We should never rely on our own understanding, but always be willing to ask God, seek His will, and obey Him. He loves us and knows what is best for us!*

From now on, **TAKE CHARGE OF YOUR FINANCES** *by being a good steward of God's resources. This means recognizing that God owns everything and acknowledging your responsibility to manage what has been given to you.*

How can you do this?

- **Break Those Bad Financial Habits**

- **Build Your Portfolio towards Financial Independence**
  - ✓ *Improve your Cash Flow*
  - ✓ *Get out of Debt*
  - ✓ *Setup Emergency Fund*
  - ✓ *Protect Yourself*
  - ✓ *Save, Invest, and Create Passive Income*

- **Plan Your Finances**

- **Understand the Power of Vision**

- **Utilize the Keys to Great Financial Blessings**

BREAKING BAD FINANCIAL HABITS

Now that you are convinced that God owns everything, you must recognize those Bad financial habits that entangle you from living your God – given destiny and be enlightened by God's word on how you can overcome them.

Looking at some of the most prominent practices that penetrate one's behavior and entrapped most to poverty, let us see how we can effectively deal with them.

Lavish Lifestyle *– Studies show that most people love to imitate the glittering rich lifestyle by mistakenly thinking that rich people spend so much on the physical stuff like shoes, bags, and cars to make them look rich. But what we should know is that most of them don't spend significantly on these; in fact, the amount of money they spent was surpassingly less than what they have. Unfortunately, many who were caught in this habit - the lavish lifestyle, is often nailed with the stigma of being "unfashionable" and would rather spend money than save just to get the latest fetish they want. A deeper root cause to this one is what we call the pride of life.*

Pride goes before destruction and haughtiness before a fall. (Proverbs 16:18 – NIV)

A lifestyle based on the pride of life will strip you of the essentials. For example, the bag you just loaned for a twelve-month, zero percent interest rate. could possibly steal your monthly deferred amortization for the down payment of your own house. The house that you and your family have been dreaming for years! Now, if you belong to this group of people, this is the right time for you to be free! The solution is simple – **BE SIMPLE!** *This doesn't* mean that you stay out of style and never dream; rather, it means **DREAM for the BIG THINGS!** Set your priorities. Consider what really matters not just to you but to your family and loved ones. Consider envisaging your family in your nice and cozy hub, watching movie in your family room together with your spouse and kids. Forget about the gadgets and other impractical things that will cause you to lose your focus on this **GREAT ENDEAVOR**. Start saving for the huge and more meaningful stuff and believe God for the best.

"No eye has seen, no ear has heard, and no mind has imagined what God has prepared for those who love him." (1 Corinthians 2:9 – NLT)

Regards for Marketing Advocate *– Filipinos are generally admired for being hospitable and warm; however, this behavior is not only limited with house visitors. Sometimes, it also includes being friendly and welcoming to those marketing connoisseurs around the archipelago. These Marketing Gurus know the see, hear & feel spot that they need to fill in every naïve individual who are a great fan of the so called – BUY BIG SAVE BIG! Unknowingly, this group of people will go rushing to the nearest mall-wide sale available without even thinking about their budget. They are not even thinking whether they are spending their next two-week allowance* *for their fare means and then wonder why they cannot even go to work because they are left with nothing. The short-sighted visionary says "It's ok because I'm living within my means"; however, this is such a big lie! Those who live within their means certainly do not realize the big picture and lack the real imagination of the future. The real thing is that we should not live within our means; instead, we should live way below our means – just like how the genuine glittering rich live! Think about the good stuff, not just the best buy. Best buys aren't always a necessity. Experience shows that women tend to fall for this marketing tactic, as most women are emotion oriented. We felt like "wow, it's cheaper" and "I must buy it now or I may miss my chance". I'm not saying men are always fine with this, but what I'm saying is that women must be more careful about this. Of course, men should by no means be enslaved as well. The next time you saw that massive billboard that says, "buy me – I'm on sale", think twice... do you really need it?*

A person without self-control is like a city with broken-down walls. (Proverbs 25:28 – NLT)

Skyrocket Investment – Our family was given several opportunities to live in and out of Japan and we were able to meet several Filipinos who have been living there in no less than 20 years. Some of them are Filipina who were married to Japanese citizens and interestingly, most of their stories are essentially the same. According to them, it was during their prime years that they send bulk of Japanese Yen to their loved ones back in the Philippines. These prime years mean that during their 20's or simply at a very young age, they started working and earned vast amounts of money as entertainers in the land of the rising sun... the time when cultural dancers, singers and other artists were not yet banned in the entertainment industry for visa. We noted several friends who, on a monthly basis send at least 100,000 Yen to support their families in our homeland. It was during the 90's so it's quite big during those times. Out of their love and felt necessity to provide, they continued to do this for many years and for as long as possible. Most of them entrusted their families back home for their investments and some, even the acquisition of real estate properties that cost them millions of pesos. With this expanse, anyone can certainly expect someone living within the millionaires' row. Surprisingly, (Bikurishita!) there was no place to go home! After many years of hard work, there was neither a single centavo in the bank nor any house in the millionaires' village. Sometimes, proceeds from their investments were already divided among their family members without their knowledge. The sad thing is, there are millions of other OFWs who may have the same sentiments as those who endowed in such a skyrocket investment. I called it skyrocket investment because it's like sending a skyrocket into the air without knowing where it will land. Individuals who are fueled by their high-income generating careers but cannot figure out the proper way to invest are those that have high probability to blunder.

My people are destroyed for lack of knowledge...
(Hosea 4:6 - NKJV)

Somebody comes along their way, gave them the idea how to invest their money with very promising high returns and boom! Before they know it, they were already part of a sprouting big time money scam!

The point is, there is no such thing as a secret investment! All the legal types of investments are available in the market and all you need to do is educate yourself with what type of investment will really fit you. Later in this book, I will discuss some of the existing investment options that are available in the market, and I hope that it will help you to start growing your hard-earned money.

Vices *– Depending on anyone's point of view, several types of vices can be considered; however, let me speak about the vices that can be easily recognized such as smoking, alcoholic drinking, and womanizing. Aside from the fact that these depravities are bad for your health and* can also greatly affect your relationships with your loved ones, these are also extremely bad for your finances. Vices such as smoking and drinking could cost a minimum wage earner more than a month's worth of salary in a year; and this certainly bothers me why most of those living within the poverty line or even below that can indulge. This is not to say that it's fine for those who can afford it; definitely no. Still, I believe that those on that category are greatly suffering when it comes to this issue. You see, the probability for those who are in the middle and upper class to notice the effect of loss of finances due to vices are not as much as those in the lower class. Nonetheless, there is no justification for both parties and all must take prodigious caution against it.

The world will tell us that it is all fine to spend some on vices for as long as you can afford it; however, the Word of God is clear that we should no longer conform to the patterns of this world.

Do not conform to the pattern of this world, but be transformed by the renewing of your mind. Then you will be able to test and approve what God's will is—his good, pleasing and perfect will. (Romans 12:2 – NIV)

If you really want breakthroughs in your finances, you must stand in the truth and do what it says. I'm sure it's not easy but I have heard so many testimonies of *breakthroughs from those who were once in bondage of various vices and it's possible by the grace of God if only, we will allow Him to oversee our lives.*

Debt Dependent *– First, let me clarify that not all debts are bad. There are some debts that can work for your advantage like those business loans which are being used to finance a business and eventually produce profit or income. On the other hand, bad debts are those that cause you greater financial losses. Good examples are those loans used for buying personal things like gadgets, bags, or anything that does not produce revenue and depreciates over time. Though I think that people depending on debts for survival is mainly a result of bad financial planning and poor financial literacy, such behavior must not be taken for granted because financial freedom starts by the renewing of one's mind (metanoia). Over the years, I have seen and known people who are very fond of getting loans even with the fact that they do not know how they will be able to repay.*

> **Just as the rich rule the poor, so the borrower**
> **is servant to the lender. (Proverbs 22:7 – NLT)**

If you are always depending on debt to cover expenditures, the thing is, you will be a servant to your lenders. In the case of credit cards for instance; an uncontrolled, unmonitored, and unwise use of it will cause you piles of debt that will force you to do everything within your means to pay them even if it cost you your convenience, loved ones, and even your health. People who practice this behavior are most likely into kiting – a legal term which is used to describe the fraudulent use of a financial instrument such as a check to obtain additional credit that is not authorized. Or in its simpler form, that is the act of drawing fund from another source of debt to cover an existing debt... and such is punishable by law. If you cannot settle your debt, the possibility is that you will not be able to save indeed. Savings are essential for investments and are practically advisable for initializing businesses that in effect can lead you to financial liberty. How then will you reach that point in your life when all your focus is primarily whom to prey for credits?

"First things first" is the key. Change the way you think about debt... **DEBT IS NOT GOD'S WILL FOR YOU!** Jesus paid the biggest debt of humanity which is the wage of sin and that cost him His own life. Do you think He would like any other debt to remain in your life? Debt is a choice and bad choices lead to death! Debt can kill you. I have seen several people who cannot find peace and had sleepless nights because debts are hunting them down. I have seen families and loved ones devastated because of piled debts. I strongly believe that this is not God's will *for anyone. He is concerned with your finances; and much more, He is concerned with your life. If you want to be free from debt, come to Jesus.*

So, if the Son sets you free, you will be free indeed. (John8:36 – NIV)

Allow Him to redirect your thinking and give you the wisdom how to get out of the trap that the enemy has set before you. I'm not saying that God will pay everything you owe and will give you instant miracles for all your problems, but I'm sure, He will guide you throughout the process and will definitely supply you with the grace that you need as you intend to recompense all those unsettled obligations; and in the end, He will be glorified because you will see His hand moving in all your circumstances.

Extended Family Syndrome *– Close family ties among Filipinos are very remarkable especially when it comes to caring for the elderly; however, the downside lies when we fail to realize that lifetime dependence on other family members can be exhausting, especially to those whom we call, the breadwinners.*

There are actually 2 sides of the story when it comes to extended family syndrome among Filipinos. The first one is those children who, even after being married because of unpreparedness opted to share houses with their parents;

unfortunately, some have brought it to the extreme level of dependence where some households include several families living in one roof together with other in-laws and children. Remember that your goal should be financial independence and not otherwise. If you intend to get married, the first thing that you should consider is to be independent in everything and this includes separating from your parents' umbrella. You must take it to your own this time. Marriage is a statement of faith that God will take care of your needs and He will be with you throughout your journey as a couple. I have confidence that the main key to break free from this type of syndrome is preparedness and trusting God for his provision. Marriage is something we must be prepared for. Not only for the wedding, but with the life ahead of it. Plan and save before tying the knot and ask God for wisdom before taking that major turning point in your life. Marriage is a wonderful blessing that was designed by God. It was never intended for our suffering because of financial issues among couples.

The other side of it is the way we look at our children. The bible is clear that children are blessings from the Lord (Psalm 127:3). This is not because we must look at them as our pension or life insurance policies during our old age; though, it is very admirable that Filipinos are naturally caring for the elderly. Children are families' treasure. They are certainly source of great joy and happiness in one's family and they should be taken care of not because we have a vision that someday they will repay us for all the good things that we have bestowed upon them. As a mother of three kids, it is of pure joy to see all our children reach their God-given destiny and fulfill God's calling in their lives. As a couple, we have faith that God will use us mightily in their lives to accomplish His purpose for them. It is also our prayer that we will be able to leave a legacy in their lives, that as their parents, God will help us to be financially independent in our old age, and we wouldn't be bothering them for any financial assistance because we believe that God is our provider even in our old age. However, I cannot deny the fact that indeed we will be so grateful if they will bless us with whatever they can because they love us and not because we have obliged them. I do believe that this is the will of God for us as parents that we should trust our Heavenly Father for His unending provision even in our old ages instead of our children.

Have faith that God will take care of everything as you rely on His grace, and He will take care of you even in your old age.

Our God is Jehovah Jireh,
"The Lord is our Provider"

Even to your old age and gray hairs I am he, I am he who will sustain you. I have made you and I will carry you; I will sustain you and I will rescue you (Isaiah 46:4 – NIV).

BUILD YOUR PORTFOLIO TOWARDS FINANCIAL INDEPENDENCE

So, how do you build an ideal portfolio?

To achieve financial independence, you must consider the following:

1. *Improve Your Cash Flow*
2. *Get out of Debt*
3. *Setup Emergency Fund*
4. *Protect Yourself*
5. *Save, Invest, and Create Passive Income*

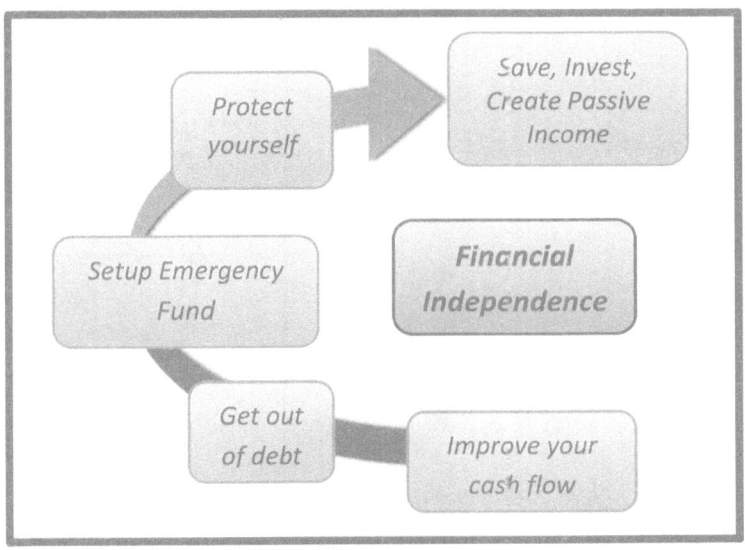

CASH FLOW COMPARISON OF THE POOR, MIDDLE, AND RICH CLASS

An important aspect that you need to understand in order to get your finances in order is your cash flow. Cash flow is just an illustration of how your money comes in and out of your pocket.

CASH FLOW OF THE POOR:

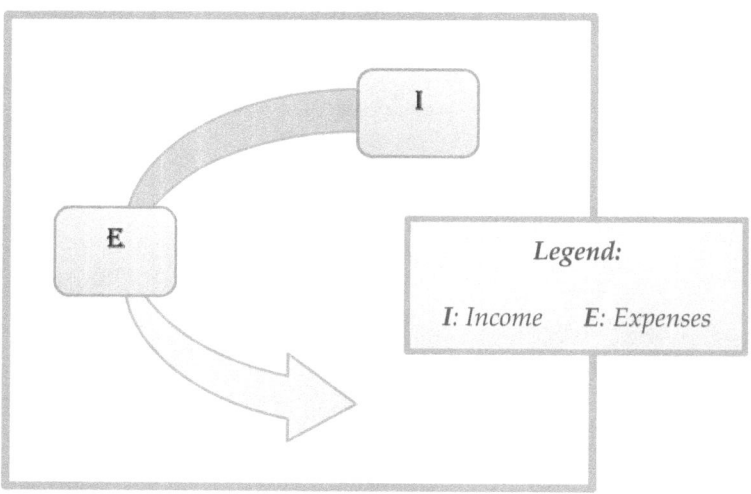

As you can see, the cash flow of the poor is income flows in, expenses flow out. That's it. Interestingly, this is when income is equal or greater than expenses; the sad *thing is most of the time, it's the other way around. When this happens, debt is likely to pile up, especially in case of emergency situations.*

CASH FLOW OF THE MIDDLE CLASS:

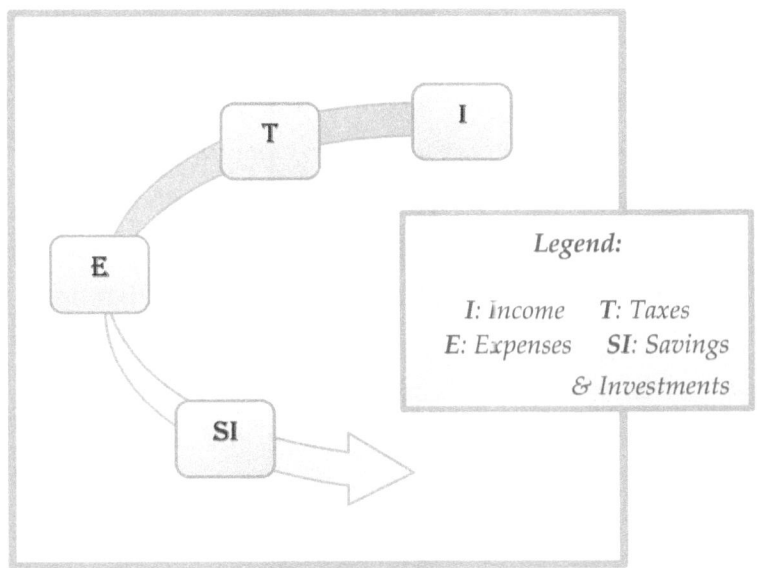

Legend:

I: Income   T: Taxes
E: Expenses   SI: Savings
& Investments

The cash flow of the middle class on the other hand involves mainly of income, expenses, and taxes. Unlike the poor which mainly consists of the minimum income wage earners and are usually exempted from paying the income tax, the middle class has no way of escaping it.

Taxes are being deducted on their pay slips even before they can receive their monthly wages. One good point is, many young professionals belong to the middle class and have the advantage of a stable income which allows them to save and invest some of their money. This is again, if income is greater than their expenses; however, most of the young professionals who came from the poor households usually felt deprivation during their younger years and there's a high tendency for them to feel the need to "catch up" and make up for the things they missed out on by buying material goods during their early years of employment, which is a prime time to build and accumulate wealth. Yes, the Middle class is the make-or-break situation where one essentially has the option to go back to his poor state or grab the opportunity to reach the next level which is to become rich. By establishing good financial habits like saving, investing, and creating passive income streams, young professionals can lay the foundation for a secure financial future.

CASH FLOW OF THE RICH:

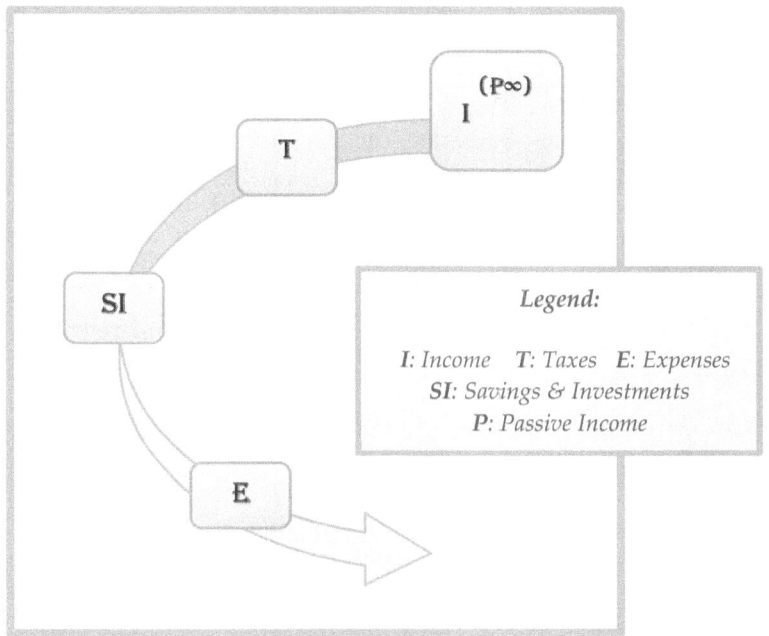

Finally, this is it! The cash flow of the rich! Merely, just by looking at the diagram, you can already see the big difference. Income is represented by an exponential infinity (∞) symbol and P which represents passive income. The main difference of the poor, the middle class, and the rich people although everyone may have sources of income is the number of streams where they are coming from.

According to various research, a rich person usually has at least four streams of income. They are in fact very good in creating passive income and consistently save and invest, which again, substantially add up to their inflows. And this is what fascinates me, they are also paying taxes; however, the question is, who pays for their taxes? In most cases, they are those who belong in the middle class. The middle class often bears a significant portion of the tax burden. As consumers, they not only pay taxes on their income, but also on goods and services they purchase, through sales tax and other indirect taxes. On the other hand, the rich do pay taxes, albeit in different ways than the middle class. They don't pay their taxes directly; their businesses represented by their companies pay for their taxes. And there's no problem with that because that's legal. You would be surprised to know that most of their businesses have even given them the privilege to reduce their tax liability through deductions and other tax strategies. And again, that is legal. And that is because businesses are good for the economy. The government thus provide incentives to encourage everyone to build businesses and help in the country's economic growth. So, would you like to be one of them?

HOW CAN YOU IMPROVE YOUR CASH FLOW?

1. Analyze your Cash Flow

Now that you understand the cash flow of the poor, middle class and the rich, I believe you can now analyze the pattern of your own cash flow; and by doing it, you will have the opportunity to improve. But how? Do it by simply connecting the dots. What I mean is, you must compare yours and the cash flow of the rich and see how you can adapt the same principle to your current finances. Sounds frightening to know the truth, right? Don't worry; the truth will set you free. If you notice, the main difference of the cash flow of the rich is the Income. According to several studies, a rich person has at least four streams of income which usually includes passive income that may either come from businesses or real estate properties, and regular additional inflows through dividends and profits from their investments; hence, this is one major area of improvement. Later in this book, I will discuss some practical tips on how to save and several options where you can invest and grow your money so stay put for a while.

2. Monitor you Cash Flow

Once you analyze your cash flow and light has been shed on how you must redirect it, it is essentially important that you monitor it so you can gauge your development while walking toward your goals and make the necessary adjustments in between. You must understand that monitoring your cash flow is crucial especially if your income is increasing. The tendency is, the higher the income, the higher will be the expenses; and if you are not careful, instead of growing, you may lose hand of it. Many famous personalities, even billionaires declared bankruptcy after putting huge amount of money on the wrong investments simply because they were not able to analyze and monitor their cash flow believing that they still have so much and not careful enough in allocating their funds; hence, I strongly advise that even with the little that you have, make it a habit to monitor your cash flow.

I suggest that you create a tangible cash flow monitoring system like an excel file or use some of the available budget applications to make it easier and more convenient for you.

3. Input Additional Sources of Income

You've analyzed your cash flow and realized it seems that if you want to imitate the cash flow of the rich, you must create additional sources of income. Not only that, but you must also learn how to develop passive income and be willing to take risk in order to invest. Of course, never ever plunge into something that you don't understand. That's why I commend you for reading this book because this is one big step that you take so you can set the proper foundation on financial literacy.

If your cash flow seems like that of the poor or the middle class, the best thing to do is of course, increase your income by creating additional streams of inflows so you can also set aside something for emergency funds, insurances, savings, and investments.

4. Control your Expenses

When I say control, it doesn't mean you're forbidden to spend. Of course, spending is simply inevitable; however, if you want to reach your goal of financial independence, you must learn how to control it. And that is why monitoring is so important. Monitor your inflows especially your outflows to know where your money is going. On the other hand, budgeting is a more active approach which allows you to know where they will go. If you can, make a good budget plan to allocate your expenses ahead and stick to it.

Some good points to remember are:

- *Set aside your savings before spending and allocate some for investments.*
- *Spend only on what are essentials.*
- *It's ok to spend on leisure if there's extra cash.*

GET OUT OF DEBT!

Another important aspect to put your attention is how to stay out of debt.

For the wages of sin is death, but the free gift of God is eternal life through Christ Jesus our Lord. (Romans 6:23 – NLT)

First, you must understand and be convinced that drowning in debt is never the intention of God for you. He actually paid for it! The biggest debt of humanity was cancelled when Jesus died on the cross to pay for the wages of our sins, and so why would anyone ever think that it's ok to have debts?

Just as the rich rule the poor, so the borrower is servant to the lender. (Proverbs 22:7 – NLT)

Second, you must understand that debts have implications; restless and sleepless nights, family feuds, broken relationships, and so much more. Proverbs says that the borrower is a servant to the lender. And when does a servant becomes higher than his master? If you are in debts, chances are, you will do everything to stay out of it. Even if you try to hide from it, it will haunt you down; hence, if you substantially know these things you will stay away from debts.

And how can you do this?

1. Understand the Difference between Good Debts and Bad Debts

What are bad debts? Bad debts are those that cause you restless and sleepless nights. Your credit card bills with piled interests that consist mainly of unnecessary spending, emergency loans, and even borrowed money for your birthday parties and major events like weddings and Christenings. If you borrowed, and you don't have a concrete or specific plan of how you can pay it back, it is considered bad debts no matter what your reasons or excuses are. On the other hand, good debts are debts that can work for your advantage like real estate investments and business loans. These loans are being made for the purpose of producing profits. That is why, finance institutions like banks set very strict rules for acquiring loans because these are expected to give them returns. On high scale businesses, loans are also essential for expansion and sometimes are also used to refinance some expenditures for recovery. However, before they can be eligible, they must have a very convincing financial statement and substantial business plan in order to make sure they will be able to pay their lenders.

The main difference between them is how they affect you. Bad debts have bad implications while good debts, if managed appropriately can work for your advantage; hence, it follows that debt, even if it's a good debt, if mismanaged, the implications can be unpleasant.

2. Use Credit Card Only When it's Beneficial

There was a time in my life that my thinking about credit card was brought to the extreme. I never had a credit card until I became a mother. I thought having a credit card will always lead me to debt, drown me, and eventually, drain all my savings. And yes, for most of us, this is so true; however, it's not always the case. Credit card is also an essential part of our life especially nowadays that shopping and even bank transactions can be made online. It gives us convenience and if managed appropriately, can also benefit us. Miles for example is one of the perks of having a credit card. Airport lounges and discounts are also among them. Again, it's not the credit card. It's the way we utilize and manage them. And once more, always remember that monitoring is necessary. You must make it a habit to monitor your spending; and because credit cards are easier to swipe, you must put stricter rubrics when using it.

3. Go to the Root Cause and Pull Them Out.

I know a famous book on finance that says money matter is behavioral; and yes, at one point, I agree with that. On the other hand, behavior is just a fruit of what's inside our hearts.

A good man brings good things out of the good stored up in his heart, and an evil man brings evil things out of the evil stored up in his heart. For the mouth speaks what the heart is full of. (Luke 6:45 – NIV)

Why do you need to realize this? Because a change of heart is a change of behaviors. And behaviors, if redirected to the proper direction can be rewarding. If you're stuck in unmanageable debts right now, you must understand what's inside your heart so that you may know which weed is causing it and delaying the growths of those essential fruits in your life. Is it greed? Deprivation? Lust of the eyes? Pride of life? How about unforgiveness?

Do not be deceived: God cannot be mocked.
A man reaps what he sows.
(Galatians 6:7 – NLT)

Just like how any fruit can be produced, a seed was planted, deeply rooted, nourished, and eventually turn into a tree that bears fruits. The question is, what seeds were planted and what are the fruits that were produced? I read a book that was written by a Master in Psychology and it was about the bad seeds in our lives; how they were planted, and the bad fruits that they produced and how to pull them off. One remarkable aspect of that book is he illustrated how the memories in our childhood greatly affect our present and future circumstances in life. Although not everything in our lives is a product of bad fruits, it is also one facet that we can investigate when we're having difficulties and troubles in our lives. One of his clients is a heavily indebted businessman who had been long suffering from ulcer and his doctor even told him that his sickness was inborn. He consulted Dr. Rob Morrissette, the author of the book (Pray through It) and *they prayed together for God to reveal a memory that may be related to his sufferings. God told them about a memory of how he was conceived; that even if his mother loved him so much, she was deeply suffering while carrying him in her tummy. As a child, he may have resented it, so they prayed together, release his forgiveness for carrying the pain while in his mother's womb and ask God to forgive him for resenting his mother. After that, he went back for his medical checkup and the doctor was surprised to know that the ulcer was gone. He was also able to manage his piled debts and little by little improved his business.*

Search me, God, and know my heart; test me and know my anxious thoughts. See if there is any offensive way in me, and lead me in the way everlasting. (Psalms 139:23~24 –NIV)

I'm not sure about what you're going through or if there's any bad fruit in your life that's causing those bad debts and troubles in your finances. You may have declared in the past that you will never be like any of your parents; but here you are, going through the same pile of debts that your parents went through, and financial troubles never seem to go away. It may not only because of poor choices in life but also because of bad seeds that were planted long ago. Pray. Ask God to reveal to you any iniquities in your heart that's blocking financial freedom.

It may be unforgiveness or resentments. Express to God how you really feel about those memories and ask Him to help you to forgive. Pray through those memories. Pardon those who have hurt you and release yourself. Allow God to move and have His way in your walk of getting out of debt and moving towards Real Financial Freedom!

4. Plan Your Way Out

Not all debt is a product of bad fruits; sometimes, they are also the product of poor choices. If you happened to have bad debts because of poor choices and wrong decisions in life, there's no way you can turn it back; however, you can always move forward and learn from them.

The first major step is to repent from those wrong motives and bad habits that are causing you bad debts. Repenting means asking God for forgiveness and committing yourself again to His will. Being a responsible steward of your financial blessings involves making wise decisions about spending and managing debt, as well as being mindful of the long-term impact of your choices. Always consult God in every financial decision that you will make in the future.

The next step is to plan your way out. I suggest that you list down all your bad debts with their corresponding amounts and ask God for wisdom how to cancel them one by one. It will be best to list them down starting from the highest to the lowest. If it's a credit card bill, start by cancelling the one with the highest amount because this is the one with the highest recurring interest.

One good point to remember is to talk to your lenders on how you can possibly spread the payment of your loans in a more favorable manner. It is always best to ask rather than hide from them.

Another thing to ponder is, if it's a personal loan, meaning, you borrowed from your friends or relatives, you may also ask if it's possible to have an x-deal with them. Say, you will do a certain task for them within your expertise for you to pay them back. Since, they're close to you, they might also consider. Of course, it depends on what amount are we talking about; nonetheless, there's no harm in trying.

Finally, commit not to get another debt while paying your existing ones. Your goal is to eliminate, remember? So don't dare get another one.

I'm sure there's a lot of creative ways out there. Pray to God. He will not pay your debts; but surely, He will provide you with wisdom and He will be with you in the process.

**If you need wisdom, ask our generous God,
and he will give it to you. He will not rebuke you for
asking. (James 1:5 – NLT)**

5. *Help Someone Who is In Debt*

**The generous will prosper; those who refresh
others will themselves be refreshed.
(Proverbs 11:25 – NLT)**

Refresh others and you will be refreshed. Sounds crazy knowing that you're also in debt; but remember, God's ways are higher than our ways. God operates in a completely opposite manner than how the world does. If you're planning and thinking your way out of debt, try to look for someone who is also in debt and help him. As you do this you will be refreshed. That's what the Word of God says.

**Give, and it will be given to you. A good measure,
pressed down, shaken together and running over, will
be poured into your lap. For with the measure you use,
it will be measured to you." (Luke 6:38 – NIV)**

Moreover, if you give, it will come back to you in many folds; so, lend a hand to someone and allow God to cause that blessing to come back to you in ways that you cannot imagine and help you get out of debt!

SET UP EMERGENCY FUND

Emergency fund is a part of your savings that you set aside in order to prepare for life's unexpected circumstances like loss of a job, illness, major car and home repairs, or even burial. It will be best if you place it in a basket that is available for easy withdrawals but separated from your operational budget or regular monthly savings.

Emergency situations can be categorized into two;

1. *Preventable*
2. *Inevitable*

hence, you must identify each emergency type to know the appropriate preparations.

I happened to be part of the Construction Department in our company and one important aspect that affects business operations and total project cost is the health and safety of workers. That is why huge efforts in ensuring them are always given in every project. In the same way, you can also apply this on your personal finance.

You must identify preventable emergency situations in your life and create risk mitigation plan. Risk mitigation planning is the process of identifying risks and developing options and actions to enhance opportunities and reduce threats to project objectives. What are your risks and what are your preparations in light of personal emergency situations?

Plan, Do, ACT *is a good way to remember a risk mitigation plan.*

Plan *– Identify your risks and plan how to manage them.*

Do *– Implement your plans.*

A *– Analyze actual scenarios (Monitor)*

C *– Input Corrective Actions (Improve)*

T *– Test the Effectiveness of Corrective Actions*

REPEAT THE PROCESS AND DO YOUR BEST TO MASTER IT!

I know someone who has four children and since their age gaps are quite close to each other, the tendency is, when one gets sick, the other three get sick also; and most of the time, the accidents they bumped into are preventable. On one instance, it's dehydration; on another instance, one was bitten by a dog. The sad thing is, they don't have health insurance; hence, debts piled up.

So, what should we do? Always remember that prevention is better than cure and a lot cheaper. It's not uncommon for families with young children to experience frequent illnesses and accidents. Knowing this as a risk factor while raising those children could have put higher safety awareness that would have allowed their parents to prepare for them.

We can learn preventive measures from the lifestyle of the Japanese. They treat food as medicine and consider them as their main source of vitamins and nutrients for their body; that's why, they put high value in the food that they eat. Healthy lifestyle is common among the Japanese society; a trait, which is very admirable. It is my prayer that you will learn how to take care of your bodies not only to be financially free from emergency costs; but also, to be strong and prepared for the calling that God has set before you.

Meanwhile, there are simply inevitable circumstances in our lives like loss of job and sudden illness no matter how we choose to stay well and healthy.

In Japan, most of the salary men are being deployed through employment agencies (haken); and although there is a high employment rate, losing one's job is still unpredictable. That is why most of the employees are covered with insurance for the loss of job so that when it happens, one can still survive for at least within 60~70% of his current monthly salary while of course looking for another job. Illnesses on the other hand, even cancers are covered by insurances to make sure that when it strikes them, they will get the necessary treatments.

Death is also an inevitable circumstance, and a memorial plan is very essential in order to prepare for any financial burdens that it will incur.

So, to top it all, emergency fund is an essential aspect at which you must consider if you want to achieve financial independence. One type of life's circumstances is preventable while the other is inevitable and we can never know which one will occur or when will they happen; so, the best thing we can do is to prepare to the best that we can.

SAVINGS:

This is an amount expressed as a percentage or portion that is deducted from your income and set aside as spare cash which can be used for other purposes such as business funds, emergencies, or retirement. Of course, the ideal is there should be separate savings for each specific purpose; however, just to make it simple, savings is the amount of money that you set aside from your income even before allocating the budget for your operational expenses. Let us define operational expenses simply as the amount of money which you use in order to pursue all your life's operation.

The cash accumulated is typically put into very low-risk investments that you can actually withdraw anytime; like a time deposit, special savings account, money market fund comprised of non-aggressive mutual funds, stocks, and bonds.

For those who are financially prudent, the amount of money left over after personal expenses have been met can be positive. For those who tend to rely on credit cards and loans to make ends meet, otherwise is expected. Savings can be turned into further increased income through investing or by venturing into businesses.

For simplicity, a mathematical equation can be used to explain a good financial report when it comes to savings,

WRONG: INCOME – EXPENSES = SAVINGS
CORRECT: INCOME – SAVINGS = EXPENSES

Make it a habit to save. And to make it a habit, one must be consistent. No matter how little the amount is, it doesn't matter for as long as you set it aside and do it consistently. You will be surprised after some time at how much possible amount you can accumulate through it. I remember during my first job how I was so determined to save even if my salary was so little. I set aside only 300 pesos every payday consistently and increasingly for 10 years and save it in our company's provident fund. After my resignation, I'm delighted to say that even though we have no separation pay, I have no liabilities with the company; more so, they gave me back the excess savings that I have after accounting all the withdrawals that I made and after purchasing two real estate properties through that. If I was able to do it, I'm sure you can do better!

PRACTICAL SAVING TIPS

1. Do it Now

Because time is the arbiter of growth, there's no better way to save than to start today. The younger you are, the better. Sad to say, I heard a lot of youngsters, even the young professionals who never dare care to save. Well, for some reason most of our young professionals came from the middle class and I cannot blame their eagerness and excitement to experience the new things they longed to have because most of them felt the deprivation during their younger years. Apparently, that's what they're thinking; however, I believe it's still subjective because this is behavioral. Money matter is again a matter of the heart. It is a heart issue. What seems deprivations to you is not at all to others. Shoes for example, during my college days, I would always long to have that pair of Nike shoes. And yes, when I finally got my work, I didn't forget about it. But here's the thing, I waited for the perfect time! I gave my first fruit to God as an acknowledgement that He is the source of everything; then, I signed up for the savings fund in our company. When I had my first bonus which was given in gift certificates, I finally bought the shoes. It's quite expensive but it didn't hurt my budget. Savings became a habit, and I did it from day 1 until my 10th year on the company *and the fruit is very rewarding. So, I suggest, start now. Begin by putting first things first. Set your priorities and put your saving habit on its top. Create a monthly budget and stick to it.*

2. Plan

When it comes to savings, planning is necessary. This time, a free-flowing system will not work for you. And since you have set a very strict budget, you must plan how to stick with it. Say for example, before, when going out for a weekend bonding with family, you don't plan your activities; hence, most of the time you were over budget, and perhaps, a budget was not even set so you spent as much as needed. This time, you must set your activities beforehand so that your budget may also follow. In this case, you will not only save money; you can also save time and energy.

3. Avoid Impulse Buying

Ladies are emotional in general and hence, impulsive in nature. I don't know with men but I have seen some impulsive men as well, so this is for everybody. Never buy out of impulse. Think before you pick! More appropriately, prepare a list of the things you really need to buy before going to the groceries or shopping malls. Just buy what you really need and never because they are on sale. And since impulses are driven by our emotions, make sure you're in good shape whenever you go to the grocery. Have a good rest and take your breakfast or lunch before going to the Supermarket to prevent you from being impulsive when buying things.

4. Be Practical

As much as possible, buy items on discounted prices. If you need to buy something, kindly determine first its significance. Do you really need it? If yes, then buy it; however, it will be better also to ask yourself if you really need it now. If it can wait, then it might be better to wait for a mall sale or go somewhere else where you can buy it on a cheaper or discounted price. Not because you are able to buy it, you will. It pays off to be practical and wise when it comes to shopping goods especially when there is no urgency to buy them.

5. Bring your bento

In Japan, bento is the term used for a meal prepared inside the house which is usually brought by Kindergarten Kids and salary men for their lunch. Bentos are popular because most of the wives in Japan are stay – at – home mom and hence are able to prepare them. In the Philippines, I believe it's so much easier because we usually have our parents or nannies within our household who can prepare for us; and if they are not around, why don't you try it yourself? You will be surprised at how much money you can save simply by bringing your own lunch at work. Instead of lining up in the canteen for lunch, use that time to have your power nap to prepare for a more productive afternoon in the workplace.

6. Be a Minimalist

Being a minimalist simply means being minimal in anything. This is as opposed to being extravagant. Say when it comes to your daily attire, how many shoes and bags do you actually need? How many watches do you really must have to know time? I used to buy as many shoes and bags as I wanted. Eventually, I realized it's hard to maintain everything and it's costly. When you have different set of watches, you have to buy different set of batteries to replace the old ones and maintain them. It's stressful. In short, buy only the things that you really need and as much as possible check the purpose of your purchase. Ask yourself many whys before jumping into that buying option.

GROWING YOUR MONEY

You're probably thinking now how to cut from your outflows after learning about savings; however, it should never be your end goal. Another important thing to think about is how to make your money grow. Once you've learned how to break bad financial habits and practiced how to save, it's time to make your money grow.

So how can you grow your money? What I'm about to show you is the door path to growing your money. I suggest that you make a thorough study on the rewards and risks associated with the following investment options through other resources. There are a lot of resources like books, seminars, podcasts, and internet-based study guides which are available for your advance learnings.

Moreover, let me say that "all investments and businesses have risks". Meanwhile, this should never hinder you from being progressive. The only one big thing that can totally hinder you from taking advantage of these investment options is fear. And fear comes when you lack the appropriate knowledge and understanding of what you're supposed to do. So, if you understand the risks and know how to deal with them, it will be manageable.

For legitimate investments, there is no such thing as easy money. Often than not, too-good-to-be-true investments are scams, so be careful! It takes time to grow your money. But it does. Sometimes others can even make it faster; so, take heart because it's not too late to succeed.

So, does money grow on trees? I don't think so; but surely, it does grow!

INVESTMENTS: *In simplified term, investment is like farming which uses the principle of sowing and reaping; however, investment is not just earning what you planted as it also allows you to grow your money in a much higher value as compared to what you have propagated. Investment is an asset that you purchased with the hope that it will generate a higher income in the future because of price appreciation. Meanwhile, one should take note that investing entails risks. And the level of risk that you can take also plays a great role on deciding what type of* *investment you will consider and how much money are you willing to let go to get your desired profit or income.*

Here are some of the Investment options which you can consider.

1. Stocks

Stock investing is a type of investment in which one partakes in one or more of the businesses listed in the stock market. Certain conditions set by the Philippines Stock Exchange (PSE) were met by these companies in order to make their companies public. Once approved, portions of their businesses were offered through Public Offering. In essence, their business is now a public business and once you buy shares from any of these companies, you become a stockholder. The number of shares that you buy signifies your portion of ownership in a corporation; hence, it also means that you are entitled to the companies' assets and earnings. Some companies even give regular dividends to their shareholders. On the other hand, we must understand that investing in the stock market means that you do not only share in the earnings but also in the totality of the business. It means, when the business is doing good you are also earning; if it's the other way around, the probability is of course, you may also have a hard time in the stock market. But if you are prudent, you know exactly what to do.

Instead of grumbling, you will look for the stocks that are below the market value but has a high probability of appreciation in the future. Stocks are very similar to the buy and sell business. Buy at the lowest price possible and sell as much as possible to its highest price.

The risks in stock market can be associated to its high volatility. This means that stocks' prices change from time to time, and one must have the proper understanding of the different strategies on how to successfully beat the market or take advantage of its ups and downs. Most of the investors especially traders depend on graphs along with other indicators to check the probabilities of a successful stock trading. You will usually hear candle sticks, open price, low price, high price, technical analysis, fundamental analysis, moving averages, etc. when you get involved in the stock market. This is if you choose to manage your own portfolio. On the other hand, some basically use the concept of cost averaging where they usually set aside a certain amount of money for savings; only that instead of putting them into a savings account, they placed them on the stock market on a regular basis and buy stocks that are on sale or sometimes they won't even care but just regularly put something into the basket and wait for some time to make it grow. They usually leave their investments for the long term, say 10 or 20 years.

One good point to understand is that one should never put his money intended for operational expenses in the stock market. That means, you should never place your grocery budget or utility budget for stocks and never treat the stock market as a lottery; otherwise, you might lose your food allowance for the month and never have anything to eat. Of course, that's the worst, but a good point to ponder before going into stocks.

In the Philippines, only a few are knowledgeable about the stock market and even those who are degree holders are not aware or have a high tendency to resist the idea of investing in it. This is mainly because we were not trained to invest. Filipino culture is focused mainly on having a degree, landing in a good company, and climbing the corporate ladder as high as possible; however, our goals to be financially independent cannot just end in having a good job and always aiming for higher salary. Our thinking should include growth.

Investing in the stock market gives us the privilege to take part on those companies' or industries' earnings due to their businesses. In the modern times, there are several brokers that offer online systems for stock investment transactions which give you the opportunity of monitoring your investments at the ease of your own time and convenience. They also offer some guidelines and conduct seminars to equip you concerning the latest market trends and give you the idea as to when is the good timing to buy stocks.

While there are a lot of things to learn about the stock market, nowadays, there are also a lot of available resources for knowledge enrichment on how you can be successful in stock trading or investing.

Hence, there is no more excuse for anyone who wants to be a stockholder. Stock investment is now so much available for everyone than ever before.

2. Bonds

Bonds are investments through loans. When investing in bonds, you are the lender (creditor) and the issuer of the bond is the borrower (debtor).

Bond is a debt security under which the issuer owes the holders a debt; and, depending on the terms of the bond is obliged to pay them interest and repay the principal at a later date termed as the maturity date. Interest is usually payable at fixed intervals - semiannual, annual, and sometimes monthly.

Bonds provide the borrower with funds to finance long-term investments; or, in the case of government bonds, to finance current expenditure.

Bonds are usually considered a lower risk investment compared to stocks because the returns are usually fixed and maturity date is predetermined; however, certain conditions vary from one to another so the best thing to do is to inquire. Depending on your preferences, you may have direct transactions with the issuing institution like banks and government agencies; however, there are also brokers or what we consider as third party that can help you in investing in bonds.

Nowadays, there are also several types of pre-need and insurance companies that offer mutual funds which promise to manage your money through stocks and bonds.

3. Mutual Funds

Mutual Fund is an investment managed by registered finance managers under a finance institution using a pool of money from different investors. The fund is then allocated in securities like stocks, bonds, money market instruments and other assets. In other words, a group of investors like you and me can invest in the stock market with the help of a finance manager. Of course, unlike having a direct broker and managing the stocks on your own, this has certain charges which are usually deducted regularly from your investment deposits. One advantage is of course, you're using somebody else's time in order to invest; say, in the stock market. You don't need to check the ups and downs and market trends, graphs, etc. because someone is doing it for you; hence, you can use your time for other things. That's why you should look for an institution that you can trust and someone you think is reliable enough to do the work for you. Of course, it's better to check the company's performance especially their years of existence. As we know, a lot of insurance companies failed to operate over time and hence have gone to foreclosures or bankruptcy, and that's part of the risks. So, it's best to look for one that has succeeded the test of time. Likewise, a professional finance consultant is very important. If possible, ask for referrals. Look for someone that has a good reputation. Someone who is not only after the marketing and referral commissions but someone who is professional enough and a bonus if you can find someone who is passionate in helping you and a real advocate of financial freedom. That is because, if you intend it for a long-term investment, you will need some advice from time to time and you will be needing assistance for any process along the way which is associated with your investment.

There are several investment options offered by financial institutions like Insurance companies which tied up your insurance policy like life insurance or health insurance to your mutual funds; so again, the best thing to do is to inquire and study the policies based on your preferences and risk factors before diving into it.

4. Metal Commodities

The manufacturing sector uses metals to make automobiles, electronics, factory equipment, jewelry, cookware, dental equipment, protective shielding, cutlery, and many other valuable items. Metals also play a role in the power and storage industries. They are important components in battery production and even play a vital role in the creation of nuclear energy. More so, precious metals appreciate overtime and because of these various reasons, they are also a good source of investment. For beginners, buying jewelries is a good start. Instead of using your hard-earned money on things that depreciate overtime like gadgets and accessories, start investing on something that has value and appreciates overtime.

For some, going into crafts of making jewelry is a good business especially if you are passionate about it. For some, putting up a pawnshop is also a good option. There are great names in the pawnshop industry in the Philippines and they are doing well. Of course, investment in metal commodities comes in various forms like jewelry craft business, electronics, and manufacturing business as big as nuclear productions. Risks may also vary from one to the other but the good news is there is an option so you can choose from which you think is suitable to your preferences. Also, if you will consider buying jewelries as investment, the way to secure them is also a challenge; so, take note of that. There are also some who invest in the open market, which is similar to the stock market, but instead of businesses, precious metals like gold, silver, platinum, etc. composed the listings. However, I'm not an expert on this matter and there are a lot of scams nowadays so please be careful with this. You may seek the experts if you are interested in this type of investment.

5. FOREX

The Foreign Exchange market, often referred to as the Forex or FX market, is the largest and most liquid market in the world; and just like the stock market, it is highly volatile.

Traditionally, foreign exchange investments were reserved for large financial institutions, hedge funds, and high net worth individuals; however, advances in technology have made it possible for anyone to invest in the currency markets online.

And like any investments, Forex also involves risks that need to be understood and managed correctly; hence, before starting your journey into the forex market, you should ensure a thorough understanding how to trade in the Forex market and the risks associated with it.

The price of a currency reflects how positive or negative the market deems the future economic health of a country or region. So, in essence, when currency trading, investors are effectively speculating on the performance of one country's economic health against that of another.

This is very similar as to how the stock market works considering the technical analysis where the behavior and movement of charts depend mostly on the market outlook. Meanwhile, various factors such as fiscal and monetary policies in each country can also affect foreign currency exchange. Inflation rate, trade imbalances, politics, and other economic factors likewise can affect its movement.

And again, just like investing in the stock market, one of the most challenging aspects of investing in Forex is to know the perfect timing when to buy and when to sell; however, instead of company shares, it's currency pairs.

Currently, with the rise of fintech, investment opportunities such as cryptocurrency, blockchain, and mobile banking are increasing; and who knows, there may be more in the future. Meanwhile, at the end of the day, there is no template, cookie cutter, or absolute rule for making any financial decision as to where to invest and grow your money. It is dependent on your expertise, preferences, and risk tolerance. The best thing to do is to learn as much as you can on each investment opportunity that you ought to get involve with until you acquire the solid and firm foundation that will help you make the most of your investing experience.

EMPLOYMENT, SELF-EMPLOYMENT, BUSINESS AND GROWTH

While cost cutting, budgeting, and savings are good, creating other sources of income is even better and it's very refreshing to see entrepreneurs who, at a very young age have already acknowledged their capabilities and passion and became successful even before having a college diploma. Nevertheless, most of us initially after graduating from college depend on employment as the main source of income and it is only through this stage where we begin to see our true passion. On the contrary, this should not be an obstacle; instead, this can be used as a bridge to enter another industry and can be considered as part of the whole learning process. After all, life is a journey and a continuous series of lessons learned. At this stage, you should have already cultivated good financial habits. To expand, you can use your talent, skills, and experience by looking for business opportunities particularly related to your regular employment. While this is the ideal, some found theirs completely opposite to their current job; meanwhile, this can still be pursued on the side, in which sometimes can even exceed one's salary and can become the major source of income. If this happens, you should not be tempted to let go of your regular work so easily. Never kill the goose that lays the golden egg; however, if enough profits have been gained from these other income generating sources, then, you can invest your full resources which includes the time dedicated to your current employment to go full time in your business. This phase is called growth. This is the point where you make your money work for you.

PASSIVE INCOME

Passive income is the income resulting from a cash inflow which can be generated on a regular basis, requiring minimal to no effort from the recipient to maintain it.

In most cases, this is where the power of leveraging operates which simply means doing more with less. Leveraging may be in the form of time, money, and other resources which may be used to replace yours and yet produces more profits.

*In the modern days, especially with the rise of digital marketing and digital entrepreneurship, a lot of business models have been developed in order to create passive income; however, let us look at investing in the **real estate** and **creating businesses** on a general note.*

***REAL ESTATE** (Real estate that generates income or is otherwise intended for investment purposes rather than as a primary residence)*

It is common for investors to own multiple pieces of real estate; one of which serves as a primary residence, while others are used to generate rental income and profits through price appreciation. The tax implications for investment in real estate are often different than those for residential properties.

Common examples of investment properties are apartment buildings and rental houses in which the owners do not utilize them as residential units but use them to generate income from ongoing rental fee from tenants. Those who invest in real estate also expect to generate capital gains as the property value increases over time.

Several lessons in economic subject will tell us that real estate is a good investment since their values appreciate overtime; however, caution should be taken also when entering this type of investment. As I mentioned earlier, there are risks in every investment; hence, you should always analyze the profitability of each investment that you intend to consider. One good thing to note when buying a piece of lot for example is to project how much profit or capital gains do you want to produce when buying it and how many years do you need to wait for the ROI (return of investment). You must also consider that taxes are automatically incurred by the government once a real estate property is purchased.

I remember when I purchased my first real estate property with one of the known developers in the country. Since it was my first time, I would say, I had several lessons learned after the transaction; however, on my second property, I did better. Don't be afraid to take risks!

Even the best millionaires in town in one way or another suffered losses. The difference is how they managed to get back on their feet and walk again. Also, sharing that experience to the young professionals inspired many of them, knowing that I was only in my early 20's when I got my first real estate property.

Investing is a choice. I could have chosen to buy my first car, but I was so focused with my financial goals at the time; and with God's grace, after some time, I was also able to buy my first car.

When you listen, you're learning. When somebody demonstrates, you understand. But when you do it, you mastered it!

You must exert courage when you do investments and businesses. A farmer doesn't expect his plants to produce crops overnight. To most of us who were not born in a rich family, we should learn, learn, learn, and try. Sometimes, you may fail; but unless you try again, you will not learn. Real financial freedom is a process, and you must be willing to undergo that if you want to succeed.

Besides, real estate investing is not a hit-and-miss or a trial-and-error thing. You must understand what you're doing, and you must set your goals. Again, plan! Planning is important in everything that you do so you know where you are and where you are going, and you can gauge your status in between.

If you want to be successful in real estate, you must be serious about it. There are several ways how to succeed but you must learn and know which path will take you there.

There are various materials available to understand the real estate business. So grab some books, watch a podcast, or attend seminars related to real estate investment and put into action whatever lesson you may get from these resources.

If you are interested in having real estate property as part of your portfolio, consider the following.

1. Establish your Purpose

Real Estate business is comprised of a wide range of options or ways on how you can earn from it. Do you want to be a real estate agent? A broker or a developer? Or do want to own properties and make it available for rentals? Or you may want to own Hotels and Resorts or Golf Courses? Set your goal and try to focus on one specialty where you can excel. Eventually, it will be easier to venture into other branches if you start by focusing on one.

2. Choose the Right Property

Choosing the right property simply means buying the right property at the right time. It entails time, effort, and expertise to look for properties which has high earning potential, purchasing it when it's all cheap and getting profit at its peak. Never do the other way around; otherwise, it will incur losses. Study the market and invest some time for research and feasibility studies. Do not rush. Find the best way to negotiate in the most favorable way possible and do the math. Never plunge into something without any computations. Finally, if it's viable, go for it. Searching for the right property is crucial in investing in the real estate.

3. Check All the Legal Documents

You may find a great property; one that has a high earning potential and one that is totally cheap. In short, it's too good to be true! And yes, sometimes, there are too-good-to-be-true properties available in the market. I know some close friends who were able to buy one. However, as

*an investor, you should be wise enough to check all the
legal documents associated with the property that you are
eyeing to buy. I also know some friends who were victims
of scammed properties like the developer cannot issue the
title even if it's fully paid because the property has
outstanding loan; therefore, it is important for you to
verify it with the "registry of deeds". You should be
diligent to check whether the seller has the right to sell the
property. Especially if the property is an inheritance, you
must check if all the rightful people have given their
consent to sell the property; otherwise, it will cause you a
lot of headaches. You must also check if taxes were fully
settled as its cost can significantly increase the amount
that you need to pay for the property in case it's not. And
just like any legal deeds, never do business based on trust
alone. Do it legally and in black and white. I know
someone who thought she was able to find a great deal and
she trusted the seller so much that she even got involved
with some personal issues and gave down payment to
settle some obligations of the seller with its existing bank
to which the property was loaned. It got so complicated,
and it was only after three years that she was able to move
in. In view thereof, no matter how kind you think the
seller is, or how well she negotiates, it's always best to go
through the legal process of buying a property.*

4. Set your Strategy

There are different types of properties available in the market especially for rental properties so you must ask yourself what particular property you are going to look for. Is it brand new? Secondhand? If secondhand, how much are you going to spend to make it pleasing and put it back again on the market? If brand new, how long are you going to pay for the mortgage and how much are you going to rent it out so you can get sufficient profits? You may also consider flipping houses which is often referred to as "build and sell". Some real estate developers started by buying a low-cost house with high earning potential. They renovate the house in a matter of days and put it back on the market and sell it within also a few days. Of course, it takes some skills to do that; nonetheless, remember that all skills are learnable so it's also a good option.

5. Ask for Help

You were never created to be all by yourself. Especially if you're new in real estate investing, it's so much easier when you have someone to ask for help. Ask someone who has been there. Ask someone with far better and stronger experience and success in the industry.

Some say experience is the best teacher; however, it's better if you know someone who has experienced it and have them share it with you. You don't have to go through all the hardships and mistakes and failures that they went through because they are willing to share it with you and you are willing to learn. If you don't know anyone close to you, attend seminars. Listen to some podcasts. You can even go to the banks, government offices, or other establishments to do your research. Try to learn as much as you can before diving in so you can maximize your real estate investing experience. When you are confident enough, go for it and apply your learnings. By this time, I trust that you will be able to establish a better strategy because of what you've heard from the ones who have gone before you.

BUSINESS

Another great source of passive income is your business. Although, particularly for startups, the probability of failure is high, we should never allow ourselves to settle on less than the best because of the fear of failure or making mistakes. Big names in the industries have been through various adversaries before they were able to build their brand; so, it is normal and acceptable that you also go through difficulties when you intend to create your own business.

A well-planned business with the right understanding, knowledge and commitment can succeed. There were those who succeeded, and I believe we can all succeed then. Now, most entrepreneurs say that your business should be one that is your passion and I agree with that because once you know what you really want to do, the probabilities are endless! Moreover, you can always educate yourself if you really want to. You may not come from a wealthy family; still, you can always go to school, work with enthusiasm, and educate yourself about creating your own business. And when you have educated yourself, commit yourself to continuously expand your capabilities to achieve success and make valuable contributions to your chosen industry. You should never stop learning because this is one great way to succeed. Again, there are several resources available nowadays and learning is no longer limited on the four walls of the classroom. All you need is the right attitude and determination to reach your goals.

Aside from dedication, commitment, and hard work, let me give you some essential advice when doing business.

1. Avoid using all your Capital at Once

I was once asked by a young professional who's contemplating on selling their condo unit; one which was initially purchased by his father and eventually fully paid by her. In order to finance a new undertaking, she wanted to sell the unit. She wants to venture in a business which she will do for the first time. She has no experience, no feasibility study, or whatsoever. This was my response. "If it's your first time, never put everything in it". Why? Because once you lose it, it's gone! And you'll never have anything to start with again. What do I mean by that? The condo unit has a good potential of producing passive income for her. That means, on a monthly basis, she can have a regular income just by doing nothing, right? That is, through the rental fee that will be generated from the condo unit. On the other hand, her business idea was good; and that is, to put up a coffee shop. The thing is, she's a newbie; hence, she has no experience. On that note, there is a probability of loss. And although that's normal for every business to have risks, one must not go into any business venture to lose. That should never be your goal. Your vision should be set to victory whenever you go into any business. I told her to hold on to that condo for passive income and try testing the water first. Rather than using a huge amount of money, I told her to use her savings; and again, not to use everything. Say, with 100k pesos, she can use the 20k to startup and study the business. Once it worked well, then she can use another 20k for expansion and growth. On the other hand, if she lost the 20k, then I'm sure she has learned something and can use another 20k to try again and this time, using the learnings that she had to make it better.

2. Learn as much as You Can and Do What Makes You Happy

Doing business means placing all the responsibility and accountability to yourself. Unlike regular employment jobs, this time you are in charge! There's no more boss or supervisor or manager who will dictate what you must do or someone who will be accountable for any decision in the office. It's all yours! Hence, the risks are all yours too! You are the one who can either make it or break it! Therefore, learn as much as you can. Do business which you are knowledgeable and something that makes you happy. Business has a lot of difficulties and challenges so you must make yourself ready for that. Business requires a lot of time, energy, and resources; and if you're not prepared for that, you might stop midway and quit the race. On the other hand, a business built with passion and purpose most likely will succeed because when the storms and shakings come, you *will hold on to them, and your dream to succeed can make all the difference!*

3. Avoid being the Jack of all Trades

It's nice to know that God put so much talent in one person, right? One can sing and dance at the same time while others can cook well and can be very gifted also in marketing. However, we cannot do everything. We just can't. I heard someone say, "I am a wedding coordinator and I also want to be a caterer so I can earn more." Too good to be true but often than not, this notion of being a jack of all trades is very dangerous. It loses our focus. If you want to succeed in business, learn to focus. If you want to focus on being a coordinator, focus on that, harness your skills, and expand. It doesn't mean you have to do everything. If you're interested in catering business, it will be better to tie up and collaborate first with other established and well-known catering services and earn through commissions rather than putting up a catering service right away. Always test the water before diving in.

Learn how to build connections and networks rather than doing everything. There is what we call leveraging which harnesses your ability to use the time, skills, and abilities of other individuals rather than yours to achieve better results. Try delegating some of your dreams and aspirations with other people who can do the job better than you. Say, if your focus is real estate construction, partner with a broker instead of you building and selling at the same time so you can focus more on building high quality real estate properties. In this case you will be able to maximize your profits and help also other people to succeed. That is what we call a win-win situation.

4. Be of More Service

I always say this, "money is not everything". If you focus too much on money and earnings in business, your tendency is to lose it. Business entails a lot of dedication and commitment and passion. Of course, technically you should earn to gauge that you're doing the right thing. However, what I'm saying is that it should never be your top priority. As you learn to focus on the quality of your products and services, partnered with the right operation system, marketing, and strategy, earnings will be so automatic. It will just overflow. And even if the earnings are not so good at first or at times, because of your consistency and passion to give the best services and products even beyond expectations, it will eventually go up.

5. Enhance your Interpersonal Skills

As I've said earlier, you can't be the Jack of all trades. You must learn how to delegate and utilize the power of leveraging. Along the way, to be a more powerful businessperson, you must also harness your skills in dealing with people. This is what we call interpersonal skills. I know that for sure some were exceptionally gifted; however, I believe that all skills are learnable. You may not be superior on a certain matter, but you can always learn and develop certain skills if you want to, especially, when you think it's necessary. In any enterprise, big or small, dealing with people is inevitable. There will always be opportunities in dealing with people especially if you're looking for growth. Manpower is vital for growth. You can't just do it all; so, it's best that you learn how to deal effectively with people.

Remember that you are now the boss so you must learn how to motivate people and empower them so they can work for you and treat the vision that you have with the same passion as you do. You must be able to drive people to work hand in hand with you. You must be able to allow your network and connections to work in perfect harmony with one another to achieve a common goal. That is why interpersonal skill is so important and I suggest that you really invest in enhancing that skill.

6. Invest in a Good Operation System and Marketing Strategy

Everybody knows McDonalds, right? How many will agree that somebody can do even better, tastier, a lot more delicious burger than McDonalds? I do. I tasted other burgers which are so much better than McDonalds. But why is its business so intense? Why do their food chains seem to have no end? Why does everybody love McDonalds? Even I, love McDonalds! Why? Because they have developed a very good operation system and marketing strategy that they were able to bring their products to the world. McDonalds are everywhere! Same is true when you do your business. No matter how good your product is, if you don't have the right system to operate and bring it to the intended market, it will be in vain. You must learn not only to produce the right products or services, but you must also learn how to create and design a very good operating system and develop an effective marketing strategy for your business.

7. Write Down Your Business Plan

The problem with aspirant businesspersons sometimes occurs when they become people of procrastination. "Mamaya na habit"(do it later), and

"Bahala na habit" (come what may). If you are serious about putting up your own business, you must take your pen and write down your thoughts and plan them well.

I've seen so many small-time businesses failed one after the other only because of poor planning. They just thought of a business, do it, then fail. End of story. Well, that should not be. If you are serious about something and you want to make it big, you must think big as well and you must start by putting them into writing.

Make a good business plan. It's best to always have a feasibility study before plunging in. Check the pros and cons of the business, the risks associated with it and how to manage them. In this case, you can be prepared and will not get caught in the middle just in case something unfortunate happens because you know what to do with it.

I did several business plans during my MBA days, and one was even accepted and utilized by a multi-billion-dollar Japanese Company. If you want to know how to make compelling and excellent business plans, contact Life Coach International Japan. I would be glad to help you.

8. Never Put up a Business based on Trust

If your intention is to put up a business, go for it. Call your friend, your brother, or your sister and build it up. But if you want to make it big time, you can't just call anyone and do business with them. Please bear with me, there's nothing wrong with doing business with family members or friends; even so, it may be better because you can easily talk to them and approach them. What I'm saying is, don't rush into things without clarifying all the conditions and boundaries for doing business. The point is, sometimes, working with closest friends and relatives gives us the tendency to overlook some important details like profit sharing, accounting, and budgeting because we trust them. This should not be. You should lay down these important matters ahead and make sure all the clarifications were set and conditions were agreed upon. If not, the tendency is, when something unfortunate and unexpected happens, your personal relationships get in the way, create conflicts, and then later forced you to drop the case and close the business. You are now left with both nothing, which involves losing your relationships and your business; and that is something you would never want to happen.

9. Make your Business Legal

I have faith that a business founded on integrity is a good business. If you can do transactions legally, then you can stand in pride because you are not hiding anything from the governing authorities. Primarily, make your business legal. Register it, get the necessary permits, and most importantly pay your taxes. If you really want God to bless you and you really trust Him that He is in control, then, you will do what pleases Him. I know that for some, this is a hard truth because corruption is rampant not just in the country, but all over the world. Someone might say, "but everybody's doing it, so why can't I?" It doesn't mean "everybody's doing it" licensed you to do the same thing. You should stand with what is biblically true and you must be convinced that as you obey His word, He is faithful, and He will bless you back.

Nonetheless, if taxes are your concern, there are also legal ways how you can minimize your taxes especially when you're running a business. All you need to do is approach a legal tax consultant. You will be surprised to know that most business owners pay lesser taxes than a regular employee; so, never be afraid to do what is right.

10. Always Choose to be a Blessing

Do you know how most successful businesses were established? Chiefly, a problem was recognized, and a solution was offered. Most of the top-performing and thriving entrepreneurs have great eyesight for the rising needs and demands of the society. They were able to get a good grasp of the underlying problems of the circulating circumstances around them and clearly recognized how to attend to them efficiently and effectively; hence, they make life better for the majority. Not only do they offer great solutions and convenience, but they tremendously offer continuous innovations that enhance the quality of life. In return, great sales and positive cash flows were generated by their businesses. So, with this, I suggest for you to always think how you can be a blessing. It is biblical and that is what God wants from us; that we serve as a channel of blessing. The good thing is, the moment we take a step of faith towards helping other people, blessings always come back in many folds more than when we released them.

Consider the real estate industry for example. Before, it was nearly impossible for the middle class and lower class to have their dream houses. Nowadays, it became increasingly possible because of the different payment options offered by many developers. Before, one must pay at least 20% of the total contract price of a property. Now, there are deferred cash payment options in which down payments can be paid in installment basis for three or more years with zero percent interest. And with that, a win-win scenario was created. Many developers have increased their sales, and in return, more Filipinos were enabled to purchase their dream houses!

Finally, who wouldn't know about Google, Amazon, YouTube, or Facebook? I think they were the best example of Luke 6:38 when they were able to provide platforms that have been able to support and enabled millions of aspirant talents, gurus, and entrepreneurs to showcase to the world what they got. The blessings come back to them pressed down, shaken together, and running over through network effect which flooded them with paid advertisements. So, choose to be a blessing!

PROTECTION AGAINST GREAT FINANCIAL LOSS

No matter how much wealth we build, there will always be some scenarios which are simply unavoidable and beyond our control, and the best thing to do is to educate ourselves on how to manage them and have a good preparation for the future. Death for example is an *inevitable circumstance and mostly unpredictable in nature. The sorrow of loss is already devastating; much more, losing the source of provision can be totally overwhelming. Meanwhile, a well-thought consideration on this matter can have a great impact on the turn of events.*

Our family has been through grief when we lost our father because of cancer; and with all the financial concerns that were acquainted to that, I would say, it's so much better that my siblings and I in general, are in a better economic state. We are professionals already and his memorial plan is all set. On the contrary, what if it happened otherwise? I can just imagine how shattering it is for those young families with seven children like ours left uninsured of their future.

Scenarios like this will strip you not only of your current finances but it can also drown you to debt just in case you happened to have no Emergency fund. Life insurance in this case is also essentially vital.

Sad to say, in a third world country like ours, any type of insurance is quite more of a burden than a security; however, you should consider that because it can save you from a huge financial loss! MRI or mortgage redemption insurance is also another significant type of insurance which secure us from paying off a part or the whole portion of the insured's outstanding mortgage balance in case of his or her death or total disability. Also, Fire insurance is essential for securing the value of our real estate properties in case of fire. On top of that, Health insurance is something that will save you from all your medical bills.

The list can go forth but the main thing here is that insurance should be part of the foundation that holds up everything in our wealth building. Just like a real building which needs a strong and reliable support for it not to collapse, insurance works in the same way.

Building a good financial portfolio is like building your dream house. An ideal portfolio includes investments and businesses that are excellent for creating passive income. These are your windows and doors, and other accessories that make your house a lot pleasing and stunning. However, in order to invest and put-up businesses, it's perfect to have savings which can be generated through a positive cash flow. Savings make up the walls and roof of the house where windows and doors will be attached. And positive cash flow can be achieved when your inflow (income) is higher than your outflow (expenses). You must also understand that most of the rich people usually have more than one stream of income; no wonder, they produce better cash flow than most people do. Finally, your streams of income are your columns, beams, posts, and other frameworks that comprise the main structure of your house. Last but not the least, firewall is also an important part of a house that protects you from sudden fire. This is your emergency fund.

On the other hand, everything on the structure of your dream house may collapse the moment its foundation was forgotten. This is where insurances play a vital role in creating a more stable portfolio; and that is, by protecting your assets which includes not only your properties but also your health against great financial loss.

FINANCIAL PLANNING

There is this saying that goes, "A failure to plan is a plan to fail". This is also true when it comes to our finances. Financial planning is something that we prepare to make sure we know where we are and where we are heading to. We often heard someone asks this – "what are your dreams?" And then, another would say "I hope I can have my own house, own car, savings, investments, etc." After years and years of hard work, what do we hear then? Sad to say, rather than success, regrets. And many times, I heard a lot of these stories from OFWs that really overwhelms my heart. However, the good news is, there's hope! Like in a basketball game, you're maybe in your last quarter or last two-minute shot; but, guess what? It's not yet game over so there's still a moment of winning! This is especially true when we put our hope in God! You would probably say, "I should have done it before"; well, yes, you cannot turn back time. Nobody does and nobody can, but we all have a future so you must decide now.

As much as God wants to help you, you have a specific part to do, and you can have a fresh start by committing your heart to God that you will take stewardship seriously and start planning your finances.

So how do you plan?

A professional financial planner is someone who gathers your data and determines your goals and expectations, analyze, and evaluate your current financial status, develop recommendations and alternatives, and help you implement those plans and continuously monitor your development towards your goals. Meanwhile, I want to put it first on a personal level because I assumed that you are reading this book because you want to establish a personal independence for your finances. It will be hard to talk about stocks, real estate, and tax planning with a professional finance planner if *you cannot even plan your monthly budget; thus, I want to ask you to apply some of the abovementioned work of a professional financial planner to your own finances right now.*

1. Acknowledge your Reality

The first thing you should do is examine yourself and analyze your financial status. Where am I? Am I poor? Middle Class? Rich? Am I living the life that God wants me to have? Am I being a blessing to somebody else and is that enough? I don't want to be so technical when it comes to the definition of terms because I believe that definition sometimes is dependent on how we see and experience them. What do I mean by that? You're maybe poor in your sight but to somebody else, you are much poorer or richer. A thing may seem expensive to you but to somebody else who can afford it, it's cheap. So, my point here is, know where you are and where do you want to go without comparing yourself with other people. Make it personal and be as specific as possible. List down and assess your financial standing in life; like, do you rent or own a house? How about a car? How's your kids' education? Do you have life insurances? How about Savings? Do you invest? Where do most of your finances go? And so on... This is the part of the process which needs a lot of honesty! Cry out to God and repent if needed. Ask God to show your actual state when it comes to your finances.

2. Set your Future

Now that you're aware of your current financial situation, the next thing to do is ask yourself, "Where do I go from here?" Is this the life that I wanted? Is this the plan of God for me? Ask God to show you His great plans for your life. Again, write them down. Make a vision board. Try to make everything look so real as if they're already happening. Be as creative as possible. Maybe instead of a vision board, make a diorama. Never limit yourself. The important thing is to positively convince yourself and shift your mind in the right direction. You may have messed it up, but God is not troubled. He is not controlled by what you did in the past or by your insufficiency. Dream again! Remember that when we think, we create!

Conceive in your mind and in your heart the life that God wants you to have. Our desires were never an accident and God has placed a special calling in your life. Now is the time to align your will with God. This is the stage where we say, "Lord this is my situation, please help

me fix it and live the life that you always wanted for me."
I'm sure God wants to help you.

3. Take the Leap

You already know where you are and where you
are heading; now, it's time to make a commitment. This
part needs a lot of wisdom so pray that you may see it
clearly through God's perspective. At this point, you
must analyze and evaluate your current financial status
and develop recommendations and alternatives so you can
achieve what you have listed on step number 2. You must
identify the following from your list:

- *What items should I retain?*
- *What are the missing items?*
- *What are the items that need Change or*
  Improvements?
- *What are the items that need complete*
  eradication?

Of course, you will agree that budget for electric
bills and water bills, house rental and kids' education
should remain in your list. But can you improve on
them? Can you limit the use of air-conditioning system?
How about internet usage? Can you lessen the budget

spent for restaurants? Can you just bring lunch in the office instead of buying? How about change? I remember, when we were young couples, my husband and I spent thousands for costly baby diapers on our first child until we realized that there's another brand which is so good and yet not as costly as the first one. We spent the same amount that we spent on our first child when we had our three kids! Wow! If only we were wiser at that time. Now, last but not the least and the most difficult part is to know which should be removed from your list. This may include a habit, a lifestyle, or something which you really love. A good example is, do you love watching movies? I mean in the movie house. If you love it but it's hurting your budget, then, let it go. It may not be for long, but it can be a good start. How about eat-all-you-can restaurants? It's ok if you have plenty of resources, but talking about financial freedom at this point, you may have to cut it down as well. How about being a travel buddy? Do you love hiking or having a vacation every month? You may also have to consider that. So, I suggest that you really think a lot and list them down; you may be surprised at how much money you can save just by cutting off some habits that you love even for the meantime until you have fully achieved sufficiency in your cash flow. I listed some items below that you can consider. Please never limit *yourself. You may have a more brilliant idea on how to personalize it to suit your financial needs.*

Items that need Improvements:

- *House Insurance, Car Insurance*
- *Electric Bill*
- *Water Bill*
- *Internet Bill, Mobile Bill*
- *Bills on Kids' Education*
- *Shopping, Groceries*
- *Fine Dining/Eating Outside*
- *Vacation*

Action:

- *Look for a more reasonable Insurance provider / Review the policy.*

- *Limit the use of air conditioning; Usage starts at 9pm.*

- *Avoid using pressurized water system during car wash.*

- *Look for a more reasonable internet and mobile provider.*
- *Prepare healthy meals for the kids instead of allowing them to buy in the school.*

- *Limit family shopping and groceries to those that are really needed.*
- *Limit family – outside – dining from four times to once a month and create weekend bonding moments, like cooking with the kids.*

- *Cancel any major vacation or out – of – the – country travel for this year.*

Items that are missing:

- *Investments, Memorial Plans, Life Insurance*

- *Business*

- *Tithes and offering*

- *Missions Offering*

- *Benevolent Fund*

Action:

- *Enhance financial literacy on this area and check what possible investments can be started this year.*

- *Look for pre-need / insurance provider.*

- *Conduct research on possible business opportunities to create various streams of income.   Some possible business ventures are:*
  - ✓ *real estate*
  - ✓ *salon*
  - ✓ *after – school, offering special classes like piano lessons and tutorial services for English and Math*
- *Use an envelope and set aside tithes every payday.*

- *Give quarterly to missions and trust God with the little that I have.*

- *Honor my parents through giving.*

- *Set aside a budget for scholarship foundations.*

Items that need Complete Eradication:

- *Vices*

Now, once you can see clearly where you are, where you are heading to, and you already committed yourself on what you will retain, add, change, improve or remove in your list, then it's time for step number 4.

4. *Do your SMART GOALS*

SMART *goals simply mean,*

S-Specific,

M-measurable

A-Achievable

R-Risk Manageable

T-Time-bound

These are the goals which you should set to achieve what you listed in step number 3.

Let me give you an example. Say you realized that you want to cut down your budget on eating out so you can save. Your SMART goal should be,

S - *Lessen the budget for eating out and turn that budget into savings*

M - *My target is to save 12,000 pesos this year*

A - *It's possible because I will refrain from joining my officemates every Friday from taking lunch outside; instead, I will just bring my lunch.*

R - *It's risky whenever I don't bring my lunch to the office; hence, I'll make sure to bring my lunch every day.*

T - *I will achieve this savings by the end of this year.*

I know this is quite hard because it needs a lot of commitment and consistency; but as you write it down, it's so much easier to see where you're heading to, and the rewards are clearly obvious if you stick to your SMART goals. Also, I'm pretty sure step number 2 is the best part; however, after that, the reality comes in and you were challenged. Don't lose heart. Do you know that in Japan, there is what they call Kaizen? It's a process used for continuous improvement and the idea is to take small step one at a time. You don't need to hurry. Small but consistent steps can bring you to your destination; and remember that as you placed your trust in the Lord, He will help you in the process. (Proverbs 3:5~6)

UNDERSTANDING
THE POWER OF VISION

What is a Vision?

Vision is a measurement of how well your eyes can see with respect to distance and clarity of a certain object of interest; as a result, the clearer your vision is, the better your definition of the object. When it comes to financial planning, your vision is defined as how well you can define your future in the area of finance. What do you see in the future when it comes to your finances?

Where there is no revelation (prophetic vision), the people cast off restraint; But happy is he who keeps the law. (Proverbs 29:18 – NKJV)

Can you specifically list down all that you want to achieve in the future with clarity? If yes, good; but if not, then you must! Vision is a bridge that connects you to your future. If you can visually see what your future looks like, it will be easier for you to set goals, bucket list, targets, etc. Vision is a summary of the bigger picture while goals are the result of analyzing your vision and breaking them down into smaller pieces so you can take *the necessary steps to achieve them. In a sense, your goals are the pieces of the puzzle, while vision is the completeness of it.*

Why is a Vision Powerful?

There is an old story about three bricklayers. Once there were three bricklayers working on a wall. When someone asked them what they were doing, the first brick man said, "obviously, I am laying bricks!" The other one said, "well, I'm building a wall." Then, the third man replied confidently and said, "I am building a cathedral for God!" Who do you think will deliver the best quality of work? When you see the big picture, you know that your labor is not in vain; and because of that, you are highly motivated, and you will give your best shot until you see the fulfillment of that vision. Knowing that you're not just waking up every morning laying bricks and building walls, going to work every day is no longer a struggle. And because you know that you are building a great Cathedral for God, you will not be living in mediocrity; rather, you will apply excellence in everything that you do. You know that at the end of each day, you are adding another effort in building something marvelous and spectacular, and you will never stop until you see, touch, and feel what was once invisible becomes tangible.

But those who wait on the LORD Shall renew their strength; They shall mount up with wings like eagles, They shall run and not be weary, They shall walk and not faint. (Isaiah 40:31 – NKJV)

Waiting on this verse in its original translation means waiting in expectation. That means, when you have a vision, especially when it's a godly vision, and you believe it will come, you will wait in expectation. You will prepare, work hard, and will never loose strength. You will always renew your strength and soar like eagles; and if faced with difficulties along the process, you will not faint because you know that something great is on its way... and that is the power of having a vision!

HOW TO ACCOMPLISH A VISION?

1. Record your Vision

**Then the LORD said to me,
"Write my answer plainly on tablets, so that a runner can carry the correct message to others.
(Habakkuk 2:2 – NLT)**

Vision board is a powerful instrument that helps you see your vision in its natural state. In a way, it is a tool used for recording what God has called you to do. I believe that everyone was called to do something remarkable while he's breathing and is expected to leave a significant contribution upon his departure from this world. Every talent that you have is not coincident. Every connection was divinely appointed by God so you can live your purpose. You are never an accident. And while these are all true, we all tend to forget; hence, recording is very important. Your vision board will remind you each day of what you are supposed to do. It will also serve as a motivation to go through life because you are living with purpose and not merely existing. It will help you set your goals and take the necessary steps to take you there. Also, a vision board will help you see the bigger picture of what's expected to happen.

In every initiative, seeing the finish product is very important because it will help you during the hard times.

We do this by keeping our eyes on Jesus, the champion who initiates and perfects our faith. Because of the joy awaiting him, he endured the cross, disregarding its shame. Now he is seated in the place of honor beside God's throne. (Hebrews 12:2 – NLT)

Jesus endured the pain and shame of the cross because He knows that at the finish line, He will be with you for eternity. With a vision board, you know what's on the finish line and where you're headed. Amid difficulties and challenges, you will endure because of what lies ahead. That is why, I encourage you to really pray for wisdom so you may know exactly what to put in your vision board; and if your vision is something that is from God, surely, He will be with you in accomplishing those dreams without any delay.

This vision is for a future time. It describes the end, and it will be fulfilled. If it seems slow in coming, wait patiently, for it will surely take place. It will not be delayed. (Habakkuk 2:3 – NLT)

And just as architects and engineers prepare architectural and structural plans before constructing a building so that they know exactly how it will be constructed, having the right measurements and material specifications, and connection details, visions are like empty dreams without any designed plans to accomplish them. You may be filled with many dreams and visions that God has placed in your heart, but after all these years, you still don't know how to make them come true. A vision board will help you organize your thoughts. From there, you can make your own set of goals and formulate action plans in order to fulfill them.

Vision boards can be done in different ways. One way is to cut out various pictures from your favorite magazines and put encouraging words to inspire you as you pursue your dreams. You can even create multiple vision boards if you want. There are no limits or restrictions in making your vision board. Be as creative as possible. Also, vision boards can be revised. If you think you're not on the right track when you first did it, you can always revise it if you really think it's needed. The idea is for you to understand and have a clearer picture of what you're called to do. I am sure that as you continuously seek God in your life, He will direct your steps and give you wisdom as you assemble all the materials in your vision board.

2. Ask God for Wisdom and Know Where the Help is Coming From

The city officials did not know I had been out there or what I was doing, for I had not yet said anything to anyone about my plans. I had not yet spoken to the Jewish leaders—the priests, the nobles, the officials, or anyone else in the administration. But

now I said to them, "You know very well what trouble
we are in. Jerusalem lies in ruins, and its gates have
been destroyed by fire. Let us rebuild the wall of
Jerusalem and end this disgrace!" Then I told them
about how the gracious hand of God had been on me,
and about my conversation with the king. They replied
at once, "Yes, let's rebuild the wall!" So they began the
good work. (Nehemiah 2:16~18 – NLT)

When Nehemiah was called to rebuild the wall of
Jerusalem, God gave him the wisdom how to go about it.
God showered him with favors beginning with securing
the permit from the government to carry out his plans and
start its construction. He was able to create a team of
skilled workers, perfectly fit to do each specific job.
Nehemiah can't just do it all by himself. Although God's
calling was for him, he was not expected to do it all alone!
Sometimes, we are so afraid to step into God's plan
because it seems too big for us; and while it is true that
it's huge, we forget to ask God where the help is coming
from. We forget that God is also a God of relationships,
and He wants us to work together especially with those
who belong to His family. God's provision means getting
ahead or providing ahead of time. It means that before He
called you into that vision, He has already provided the

means to accomplish it. You must seek God for wisdom and ask Him who are the people to ask for support. And when you do know the answer to those questions, learn how to impart to them the vision that God has given you. This is extremely important because once your team knows where you're headed, working can be so much easier and a fun thing to do together. Amidst the challenges, somebody can also lift you up so you can be faithful to what God has called you to do.

In the area of finance, maybe God has given you a vision to have your own business; and since you were not born from a family of entrepreneurs, it seems more cumbersome and elusive, thinking that you were inexperienced to take the helm. You get stuck with dreaming, and you don't even know where to start. Meanwhile, take heart! If the calling is from God, then believe that God has provided ahead of time. Pray for wisdom and seek for help. You may not be well versed in business, but God can provide somebody to help you during startup; or, God can give you the wisdom how to enroll in a business school and provide you with sufficient finances so you can pursue a degree that will enhance your skills in entrepreneurship. I'm not sure where or how God is going to do it in your life but I'm sure that He is able!

3. Create a Plan

My husband would always tell me this, "a vision without a plan is just a dream". Until you develop a plan how to achieve the vision that God has placed in your heart, it will just remain as a dream which may or may not happen - like hitting the moon with the fist. Of course, God is gracious, and nothing is impossible with God; however, God wants you to participate in His plan. God is a relational God. Just like a father who loves doing things with his children, God loves it when we participate in His agenda. He placed a vision in your heart, and He will give you the wisdom how to do it and He will copiously give you the ability to do it! Your first step is to plan. And how will you do it? First, you must set your goals based on your vision board. Ask yourself what sets of goals should you established for you to attain your vision. In short, break down your vision into smaller pieces. And from those pieces, create action plans. What are the specific actions that you must take for you to achieve each goal?

Remember your smart goals? SMART stands for specific, measurable, attainable, risk – manageable, and time – bound goals which we discussed in financial planning. In a way, goals will give you a sense of urgency because they entail time. For some, this is hard; but to some, this is exciting! I hope that you choose the latter one. Always remember that if others made it, you could also do it and you have what it takes! You are blessed with all the gifts and talents perfectly tailored for your calling. All the connections that you have were divinely appointed by God, and if God called you to it, surely, He would see you through it!

You're maybe wondering, "How can I believe that when I am deeply drowned in bad debts?" Or, "how am I supposed to do that when I don't even have a single cent in my pocket to start my own business?" "I don't even know how to save." Yes, you may have all the valid reasons to doubt; but unless you try, you will never know. Come to think and go back to Chapter 1 and take the Word of God seriously about the truth concerning finances. Remember that God is the owner of everything. He can bless you and all you need to do is trust Him. Trusting Him means allowing Him to work in your life through obedience. Live by the truth of His Word, do what it says and see and taste that the Lord is good!

"God's love is unconditional, but we can only receive the fulfillment of His promises within the premise of faith and obedience."

4. Be Faithful to the Vision

Fight the good fight of the faith.
(1 Timothy 6:12 – NIV)

When you made your vision board, everything seemed so nice and cool; however, the moment you break down the puzzle and check down the littlest details which include your goals and action plans, you begin to doubt and probably go back to your vision board and ask if you are really called to do that. You begin to feel upset, and fear starts to creep in, thinking that it's just too big for you. When this happens, it's now the perfect time to remember that faith counters fear. And faith is not just having faith in your heart, but faith is an action word that says fight! Fight the good fight of faith! As you choose to never settle for less than what God has called you to do, there will be battles in between and you need to fight. Never allow the opinions of faithless people to determine your future. Never give them the opportunity to influence you. Release your faith by doing what you are called to do.

If you happen to be reading this for the first time and are in serious financial turmoil, you're probably wondering what to do. But instead of overthinking, I suggest that you do something about it. You'll never know what will happen if you don't take a step. Keep in mind that those steps, even though little, can take you there. Don't stop in the middle. Continue to the finish line until you see the reward. The effect of setting aside some portion of your monthly salary to save may not show an immediate impact on your finances; but as you choose to do it regularly and consistently, holding on to the grace of God to be disciplined and committed to be financially free, I am explicitly sure that one day you will reap the fruits of your labor if you do not give up!

KEYS TOWARD
GREAT FINANCIAL BLESSINGS

While savings, investments, and passive income are great tools to make you wealthy, are you aware that there are also other keys that can unfold great financial blessings in your life?

For those who will read this for the first time, this may look like a labyrinth; nonetheless, remember that God's ways are higher than our ways and His thoughts are higher than our thoughts, and it's only through taking actions that we can exercise our faith for what we truly believe.

1. Bring your tithes into the store house.

Giving our tithes is not an act of levy to God or acquiescing to some religious obligation. Again, tithing is a matter of the heart. It brings us closer to the right focus in which our worship was directed to our God and not towards our material possessions. If we truly believe that God is the owner of everything, tithing should never be a burden. It will be a lifestyle. Nonetheless, this is the only command that allows us to test God. Isn't that a wow?! God has given us the privilege to test him! In what way?

Bring the whole tithe into the storehouse, that there may be food in my house. Test me in this," says the LORD Almighty, "and see if I will not throw open the floodgates of heaven and pour out so much blessing that there will not be room enough to store it. (Malachi 3:10 – NIV)

Subarashii! I started tithing during college and I can say that God has been so faithful with His Word. I cannot remember a time when I was able to outgive God. Never! Even when I got married and have kids, His provisions are never ending; favor upon favor overtakes us, and not only that we were blessed by God, but God even made us a channel of blessing to the people around us. Therefore, bring your tithes and allow God to pour out His overflowing blessings into your lap.

2. Give beyond your tithes.

Tithing is something that we give back to God; and because it really belongs to Him, there should be no more negotiations about it. On the other hand, giving means giving beyond our tithes and drawing from what we have been entrusted.

Give, and it will be given to you. A good measure, pressed down, shaken together and running over, will be poured into your lap. For with the measure you use, it will be measured to you." (Luke 6:38 – NIV)

Yes! Give more and you'll have more. That's what God says in His Word and believe it because God is faithful. I remember a lot of times in my life where God helped me to stay peaceful and never runs out of provision amid uncertainties and new beginnings. When my husband and I got married, we were still on the rank-and-file level in our company. Our generous wedding sponsors blessed us with so much, but in one of the church services about sowing and reaping, I sensed that God was inspiring me to believe Him and sow our wedding monetary gifts in the missions offering. We obeyed God's leading and in just a matter of months, my husband got an overseas assignment which allowed the whole family to stay with him. We brought our first child to Japan; and in the same country, I gave birth to our second child. In just a month, the amount that we received from my husband's work far outweighed the amount that we gave to the missions offering. Wow! And it's not the first time God ever told us to sow in advancing His Kingdom; nonetheless, it was not the first time we ever experienced God's abundance through giving. Matthew 14:13-21 illustrates how God was able to feed more than five thousand people by responding to the faith of a little boy who gave up his five loaves and two fish. When God asks us to give something to him, it's never because He needs our money; instead, He is preparing our hearts so we can receive something greater from Him. Everything that we placed in God's hands, He multiplied more than we have ever thought or imagined!

3. Lend to the Poor

I know it's overwhelming and sometimes even upsetting when somebody borrowed and never pays at all. Or sometimes, it's frustrating when we always give and never been reciprocated or even thanked for our good deeds. Nonetheless, take heart! God knows our labor of love and it will never be in vain.

Therefore, my beloved brethren, be steadfast, immovable, always abounding in the work of the Lord, knowing that your labor is not in vain in the Lord. (1 Corinthians 15:58 – NKJV)

Does it mean God is ok with debt and ungrateful people? Of course not! Certainly, that's not what it means because God paid for the biggest debt of humanity and gave himself as a ransom for our sins. The reality is, there will be times when people, even those who are closest *to us will fail us in the area of finance; however, our eyes should be focused on the Lord who always rewards us for our every good deed. We may not see the reward at once, but God will surely give it because He is faithful; that if we lend to the poor, we lend to God and He will repay us.*

> **If you help the poor, you are lending to**
> **the Lord— and he will repay you!**
> **(Proverbs 19:17 – NLT)**

Who then are the poor people? Those are the ones that cannot pay us back for extending our financial support. It doesn't mean we must blindly give to anyone, but we must be willing to extend our hands to those who are in need. They could be our friends, relatives, or even strangers; especially, those who are in the side skirt of the society. Those who cannot really pay us back are the poor people; and with our generosity as an act of worship to God, He promised that He will pay us back. And when God pays us back, it surely comes in many folds!

Chapter 3

THE PURPOSE OF BEING
RICH & FREE

*You will be enriched in every way so that you can be
generous on every occasion, and through us your
generosity will result in thanksgiving to God.
(2 Corinthians 9:11 – NIV)*

If being rich doesn't necessarily mean being free, why then should you desire growth in your finances? It's because God wants you to live with a purpose! While being rich doesn't necessarily entail freedom, a prosperous man with a noble purpose creates the big gap.

"The clearest meaning for being rich is the gift of purpose and significance."

God wants to bless you in every way and even in the area of finances so you can be a channel of blessing. Through you, someone will realize that somebody cares for him. You will be God's ambassador to the lowly and hurting, and you will be his hands reaching out to those that cannot create opportunities for themselves. God desires to bless us; however, our wrong motives can get in the way and blocks those promises that were already given to us.

When you ask, you do not receive, because you ask with wrong motives, that you may spend what you get on your pleasures. (James 4:3 – NIV)

While God can prosper us, He is much more concerned with our hearts. Sometimes, a state of overflow can also pull us back; instead of leading us to God, it can also cause us a lot of heartbreaks and dissatisfaction. Into some extremes, it can even lead us to emptiness, depression, and death. If you really want to have breakthrough in your finances, allow God to examine your heart and fill it with the right motives. Motives that are pleasing and aligned with His will. You can do that by delighting yourself in the Lord.

Take delight in the LORD, and he will give you the desires of your heart (Psalm 37:4 – NIV)

I encourage you to yield your desires to God and allow this lesson to be deeply rooted in your soul. For it is only when you truly know your purpose that you can really experience the fullness of joy of having God's blessing in your life!

LOVING AND GIVING

I remember a saying that goes, "you can give without loving but you cannot love without giving". Love implicitly requires giving. Whether time, energy, or other resources, it will essentially require you to give something. The fullness of God's love for us was shown by giving His most precious possession; that is, His One and only Son Jesus Christ. He gave it all... And that is love!

Now, you have your mind set on the right direction, you have your savings, investments, businesses, and protection against great losses; hence, what's next? Travel? Enjoy? Retire? Yes, as good as it sounds, and nothing is wrong with enjoying life as it is the will of God for us.

However, real freedom is a life focus not only on loving ourselves. A life of freedom includes sharing the love that we received; and that includes, our financial blessings. God's will for us is to be a channel of blessing. And if you must love, then you must also give.

Wherever your treasure is, there the
desires of your heart will also be.
(Matthew 6:21 – NLT)

Where do you focus your giving? That is where your heart goes.

Remember, naked are we when we came on earth; and naked, we will depart. At the end of the day, we will leave everything behind us and all that will be left are those that have eternal value. How do you use your financial blessings? Do you use it only to gratify yourself? Do you faithfully bring your tithes and offerings back to God? Have you ever touched somebody else's life because you gave? Have you ever helped someone who's starving? How about those who are sick in body? Have you done something to ease their pain through giving? Again, love requires giving. Have you ever truly loved?

On the other hand, remember that charity begins at home. How do you treat those who are near to you? Your parents? Your brothers and your sisters? Or are you better off with friends?

But those who won't care for their relatives, especially those in their own household, have denied the

**true faith. Such people are worse than unbelievers.
(1 Timothy 5:8 – NLT)**

I know it's so much easier said than done; but this is what love truly is. Love requires giving.

One big thing I realized is that our time on earth is very limited. Love while the people you want to love are still breathing. Tomorrow may be too late. Give while they can still enjoy it and not when they are on their deathbed. Yes, it may sound morbid but it's true. After God, love your parents. They loved you and they deserve you to love them back. Love your siblings while you still can. It's hard to grow old alone. I have seen how blessed we are as a nation to have siblings by our side. Our economic condition may not be as rich as Japan or other first world country, but the family that we have is already a treasure that we can be thankful for; therefore, if you have the opportunity to practice love in your home because you have somebody to share it with, be thankful. Treasure, cherish, and love your family.

Finally, love others.

"When you harvest the crops of your land, do not harvest the grain along the edges of your fields, and do not pick up what the harvesters drop. Leave it for the poor and the foreigners living among you. I am the LORD your God." (Leviticus 23:22 – NLT)

Do not harvest everything. Leave some to strangers and give some to those who are less fortunate. Give some to your friends, to your servants, and to your neighbors. Never keep everything for yourself. A life of surrender knows how to give. What we received from the Lord is overflowing and we cannot keep it all to ourselves. As the song goes,

"So blessed, I can't contain it. So much I've got to give it away; your Love has taught me to live now... You are more than enough for me!" - One Day by Hillsong

THE BENEFITS OF GIVING

1. It Gives Refreshment to The Soul

The generous will prosper; those who refresh others will themselves be refreshed.
(Proverbs 11:25 – NLT)

It feels so good when we give. I believe in one way or another, you have experienced giving and I'm sure you felt the same way too. When we truly give, our souls are being refreshed. There is something within us that spark when we give. I believe because we were designed by God to be like that. God's original plan is for us to be blameless and pure. It was only when the first sin came that we became corrupted. More so, when we have Jesus, we have the heart and mind of Christ. That's why it feels so good when we give because He lives within us. There is a relief in our soul when we touch others through our giving.

I remember I was so tired from work, and I really wanted to rest by having a seat in a bus; however, an old lady stands in front of me and I just can't resist the conviction to offer her my seat. I gave it and she was very thankful. She even told me several times "Domo arigatou gozaimasu", which is a very polite form of saying thank you in Japanese. I was so tired, but I just cannot explain the joy that it has brought me. I was thankful to God for the opportunity to be a blessing. I believe that the love of God compels us to do good things and it refreshes our soul. Why don't you pray and ask God for an opportunity to give and find out how it will bring refreshment to your soul?

2. *It Brings More Abundance*

***One person gives freely, yet gains even
more; another withholds unduly,
but comes to poverty.
(Proverbs 11:24 – NIV)***

That's just the way it is. God's ways are so much different from the world. The world will say, take, take, take, while the Word of God says, give, give, give. It sounds crazy to many but to those who put their trust in the Lord, this is real. And it's so real I'm sure because I know. And I know because I've experienced it in so many ways and I realized you can never outgive God!

I love branded perfumes, bags, cosmetics, and watches; but the thing is, I never want to spend too much on them, and I prefer to give my tithes and my offerings. However, God is so great! There were times when I wouldn't buy perfumes for five years because a lot of friends and loved ones gave me at least one. Watches? Latest phone and branded bags? I have them all genuine and guess what? They were all gifts! Again, I have them, not because I'm good, but because God gently touched someone's heart... God doesn't owe anything to anyone, yet in His great love and mercy and abundant grace, whenever we give, He always makes sure, we receive something greater.

On the other hand, real abundance from God is not only in the form of finances. Great Health is a blessing. Do you know someone who is so rich and yet so sick? I'm sure you read about famous entrepreneurs and wealthiest businessmen who realized that the amount of money they had doesn't really matter on their deathbed. Joy is also a great blessing. Ever heard of the famous bag founder who committed suicide? Depression kills and money cannot save you. Only Jesus can!

So, what's the connection between giving and abundance? Giving, especially giving back to God in tithes and offerings are one way of saying, "God, I trust you with all my heart". I believe it's easy to trust God with other things, but it is in the area of finance that you can really test your faith if you really trust Him that He is the owner of everything, and that He loves you, and He will take care of your every need. Yielding your finances to God is saying that real abundance comes from the Lord, and you are not putting your trust on money to have it. Real abundance comes when you know that God is in control, and His grace is sufficient, and He will see you through.

What is in your hand that is holding you back from having real abundance? Why don't you give it to God and allow Him to multiply it in ways that you cannot imagine? If God was able to send His One and Only Son and gave up His life so He can redeem us, why wouldn't God give you your daily bread, your joy, your peace, and a life of abundance?

3. It Brings Glory to God

You will be enriched in every way so that you can be generous on every occasion, and through us your generosity will result in thanksgiving to God. (2 Corinthians 9:11 – NIV)

Our giving results in thanksgiving to God! No one will ever believe anyone with the gospel until they experienced it. What do I mean by that? Sometimes, we wanted to share to our friends, loved ones, and even strangers how much God cares, how Jesus died for them, and how great God's love is; but unless they saw it in you or experienced it in a more tangible way, they will never believe you. God wants to bless you so you can be a blessing not only for some of the time, but God says, on every occasion! Why? So, they can feel the love and compassion of God in a more concrete way and eventually realized that God has been caring for them and loving them all along. They will realize that God hears them because they experienced God's blessings through you!

Believe it! God wants to bless you and He wants to bless other people through you! He is just looking for the person with the right heart; a person who is passionately loyal and committed to accomplish His purpose.

Your giving brings glory to God; hence, choose to be a blessing!

ON BEING A BLESSING

A life full of blessings is good, but life as a blessing is even better. The good thing is, when we learn how to bless others, we feel empowered too. God's promise is that if we are faithful in the little things, God will entrust us with more.

So, how then can we become a blessing? There are three things I would like to share with you.

1. Pray

Did you know that time is something so precious that once it's used it's gone? Unlike other resources which can be retrieved, recycled, or recreated, time is a nonrenewable resource. When we pray, we give our precious time for someone else. We bless them when we lift their concerns to God. The good thing about prayer is, as we intercede for other's needs to be met, we also commune with God. We also receive from Him because prayer is a two-way type of communication. God hears us and He also speaks to us. He also blesses us while we bless others. That's just the way God works. He always makes sure He blesses us. Not because we are good or deserving, but because He is righteous. So, if you want to be a blessing, learn to pray for someone else.

2. Go

It's a good thing to pray and lift our concerns to God; but sometimes, we are also called to go. Go means using our own strength and efforts to do something that needs to be accomplished. If charity is in your heart, you could literally join in the charity works, feeding, serving, and meeting face to face those who are in need. I know a lot of missionaries and they are literally and physically present in the mission field. That's what missionaries do. They make themselves available for the works of God.

In your case, what is in your heart that you can do to bless others? It may be teaching and feeding less fortunate kids, helping in the community environmental projects, serving the church, or just talking to somebody who needs a smile and a hug and words of encouragement. To somebody else, a pat on the back means so much more than you can even think or understand. Going means being available for others. Look for someone and bless them. I believe that every day, God is leading us to bless and do something good for others.

3. Give

As much as we want to be there - where we want to be, the reality is, sometimes we cannot. It's understandable that we can't always be there so the best thing to do is give. Giving gives us the opportunity to send others who can go and still accomplish the same purpose that we have in mind. Again, this is what we call leveraging. We allow others to accomplish what we want to accomplish even if we can't be there physically; hence, earn as much as you can and give as much as needed. You see, real financial freedom is not about putting emphasis on your barns and satisfying yourself. Real financial freedom comes when you are willing to maximize the gifts, talents, and abilities that God has given you and use it to fulfill His very purpose by showing his love, compassion, grace, and mercy to those who need it. And who doesn't need those anyway?

When we learn how to be good stewards of His great financial blessings, we can have more time to spend in prayer. We can have more time to go where he wants us to go and we can give more because it's overflowing. That is real financial freedom. That is the fullness of God's blessing! It never stops with us. Otherwise, we will be like the Dead Sea who happens to be what it is right now because it never flows. It becomes dead the moment it stops flowing. Blessings are like that, and I believe we are called to do that.

If you want real financial freedom, learn how to be a blessing. Desire to be like one. Be passionate to earn more so you can give more. Living a blessed life becomes alive in us when we choose to be a blessing!

I realized in my walk with God that as we focus on the blessings, we are withholding them; but when we focus on the One who blesses us and His purpose for the blessings, they just flow supernaturally.

Again, God desires to bless us so we can be a channel of blessing. It is when you purposefully live your life that you can really find satisfaction and significance. Satisfaction and significance immersed when you know what you are called to do, and you are passionately doing it. Certainly, your identity should never mix up or should never depend on what you're doing because you are already priceless in the eyes of our Creator. What I'm saying is that you are created for a purpose, and you are called to live a life of significance. When you are overflowing in the area of finance, you have a great calling, and you also have a great responsibility to the society.

When someone has been given much, much will be required in return; and when someone has been entrusted with much, even more will be required. (Luke 12:48 – NLT)

I believe not everyone was called to be a CEO or a President but I'm sure God has called you to be a channel of blessing; and whatever your position in life, God still called you to be financially free – not lacking in anything. And if you will continue to seek God and His will, He will lead you and guide you on the way that you should go. He will show you not only how to be free, but to be overflowing, so that in every season, you can reflect the very character of God; a God whose steadfast loving kindness never ceases.

ENJOYING LIFE

Finally, while it is God's will for you to be a channel of blessing, it is also God's will for you to enjoy the life that He has given you.

Moreover, when God gives someone wealth and possessions, and the ability to enjoy them, to accept their lot and be happy in their toil—this is a gift of God. (Ecclesiastes 5:19 – NIV)

Why do I have to include this topic? It's because I don't want you to go to the extreme. Anything that is in extremity is not from God.

It is good to grasp the one and not let go of the other. Whoever fears God will avoid all extremes. (Ecclesiastes 7:18 – NIV)

I remember, I was so determined to be financially free; hence, most of the time, I deprived myself of the good stuff. I worked hard, I give more, but I forgot to treat myself even if I can afford it.

I praise God for my husband. God made him especially for me. He taught me how to be practical and enjoy the fruits of my labor in a way that pleases God. He taught me how to enjoy the beautiful creation of God by travelling and going to places I could have never been if only by myself. While I am very good at saving and making investments, my husband is very good at purchasing and I'm not kidding; he is very good at purchasing items at very reasonable prices. I believe it's a gift and that's why we're perfect match!

I encourage you today to live life. Allow God to breathe life into your life! Many are just breathing but are not truly alive. When you have God, you have everything! And God is not cheap. He is not even boring. He is a God who provides and allows his people to enjoy His blessings. If you're like my personality, someone who is quite homebody and not so gifted at maps and directions but would love to try new things but just don't know how or where to start and still single, pray for a perfect match. Ask God to give you the discernment whom to marry. I know we're talking about finances here and not marriage but marrying the right person is just another make or break situation that can also bring great impacts on your finances; hence, marry the right one. You may go through a lot of mistakes in life but try to be good at two things: choose whom you will serve (Jesus) and whom you will marry. I assure you; it will save you from a lot of life's hurts and pains.

So, enjoy life. Enjoy it with your family, friends, and loved ones. Enjoying doesn't always mean extravagant and expensive; but surely, it will incur cost. If you're financially free, learn to set aside some budget for your leisure. Investing doesn't only mean investing in finances. Invest also in the welfare of your body and soul. Invest in your kids, soon they will be all grownups; enjoy them while they're young – while you can still tickle their faces and kiss them and hug them. Invest in your parents; someday, they will be gone. Enjoy your marriage; that person is God's gift to you. And if you're single, enjoy your time of waiting. Never rush because God is preparing something spectacular for you. Finally, enjoy your walk with God. Talk to Him every day. I'm sure, that will be your biggest and most profitable investment of all time!

CLOSING REMARKS

Thank you for allowing me to participate with you in your goal towards achieving real financial freedom! It was a nice experience to be with you in this voyage!

I hope that this book has brought some light into your life and gave you understanding on how you can manage your finances the way God has planned for you. For some, this is just the beginning, while for others, a wakeup call; nonetheless, I yearn that it breathes freshness to your mind and gives audacity to your soul that there's hope and it's never too late to dream again.

I am in deep faith that as you seek His guidance, you will see greater things beyond your dreams and imagination. He will take you to places you have never been and will show you great compassion and favor in everything that you do, and you will see not only freedom but breakthroughs in your finances and make a difference in somebody else's life!

May God richly shower you with His love and grace in every area of your life and may you give glory to the One who gives us the ability to triumph! In Jesus Name, Amen.

FOR COLLABORATIONS, SEMINARS, WORKSHOPS, & WEBINARS

(Churches, Corporations, & Organizations)

Contact

Life Coach International Japan

FACEBOOK PAGE:

Life Coach International Japan | Facebook